EASY PIANO

IRISH FAVORITES

Arranged by CAROL KLOSE

ISBN 978-0-7935-2177-7

HAL•LEONARD®
CORPORATION
7777 W. BLUEMOUND RD. P.O. BOX 13819 MILWAUKEE, WI 53213

EASY PIANO
IRISH FAVORITES

8   BELIEVE ME IF ALL THOSE ENDEARING YOUNG CHARMS

4   DANNY BOY (LONDONDERRY AIR)

11   GALWAY PIPER, THE

14   GARRYOWEN

17   GIRL I LEFT BEHIND ME, THE

20   HARP THAT ONCE THRO' TARA'S HALLS, THE

26   HARRIGAN

28   HAS ANYBODY HERE SEEN KELLY?

23   HAS SORROW THY YOUNG DAYS SHADED?

30   IF I KNOCK THE "L" OUT OF KELLY

33   I'LL TAKE YOU HOME AGAIN, KATHLEEN

36   IRISH WASHERWOMAN, THE

38   KATHLEEN MAVOURNEEN

42   KERRY DANCE, THE

45   KILLARNEY

48   KITTY OF COLERAINE

54   LITTLE BIT OF HEAVEN, A (SHURE THEY CALL IT IRELAND)

51   McNAMARA'S BAND

56   MINSTREL BOY, THE

58   MOLLY MALONE (COCKLES AND MUSSELS)

62   MOTHER MACHREE

60   MY WILD IRISH ROSE

68   RORY O'MOORE

72   ROSE OF TRALEE, THE

76   SWEET ROSIE O'GRADY

78   'TIS THE LAST ROSE OF SUMMER

65   TOO-RA-LOO-RA-LOO-RAL (THAT'S AN IRISH LULLABY)

80   TOURELAY

86   WEARIN' OF THE GREEN, THE

83   WHEN IRISH EYES ARE SMILING

94   WHERE THE RIVER SHANNON FLOWS

90   WHO THREW THE OVERALLS IN MISTRESS MURPHY'S CHOWDER?

DANNY BOY
(Londonderry Air)

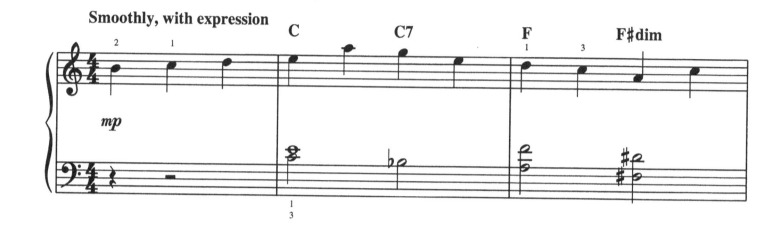

1. Oh,   Dan - ny   Boy,   the
2. See additional lyrics

With pedal

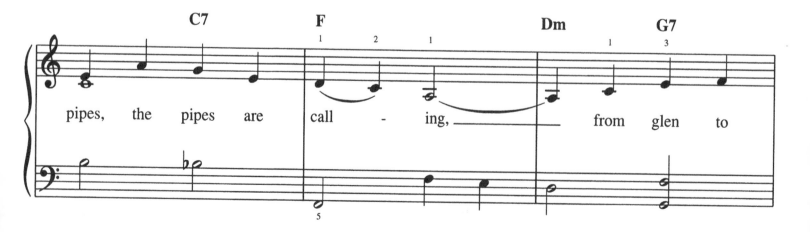

pipes, the pipes are   call - ing,   from glen to

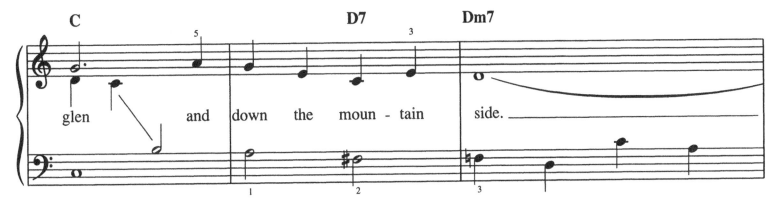

C   D7   Dm7

glen   and down the moun - tain   side.

G   C   C7

The sum - mer's gone   and   all the ros - es

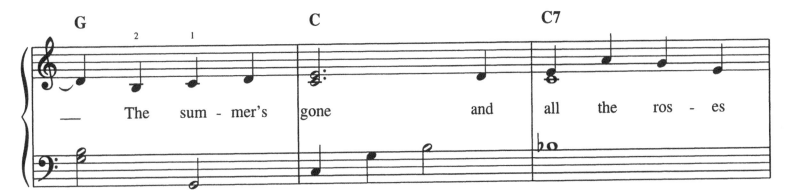

F   Dm   Fm   C/G

fall - ing;   'tis you, 'tis   you   must

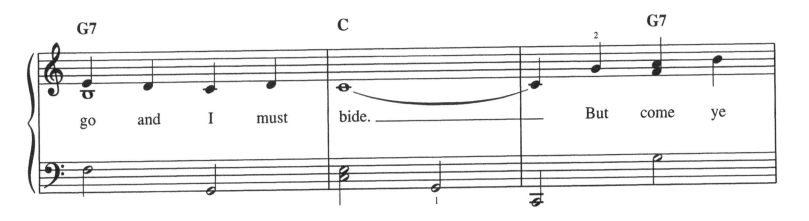

G7   C   G7

go and I must   bide.   But come ye

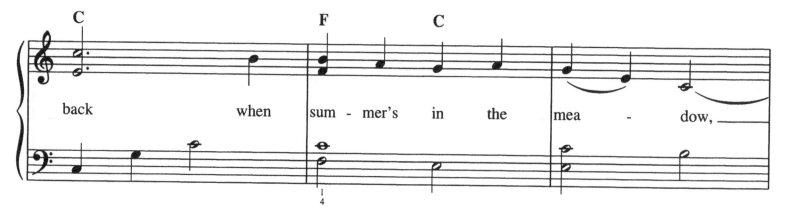

back when sum - mer's in the mea - dow,

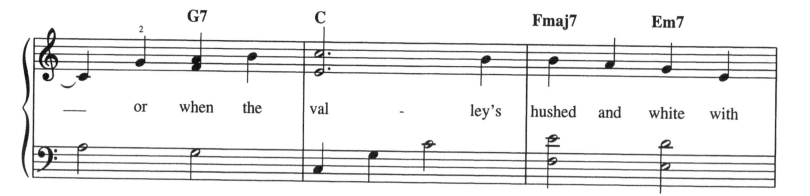

— or when the val - ley's hushed and white with

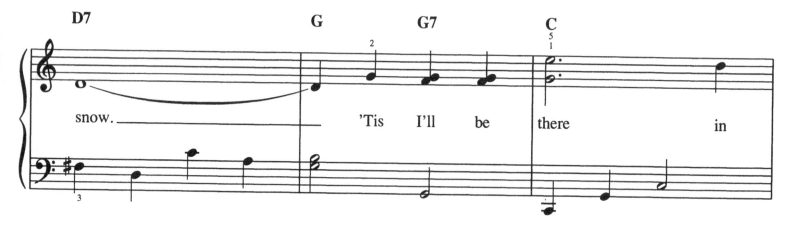

snow. 'Tis I'll be there in

sun - shine or in sha - dow. Oh, Dan - ny

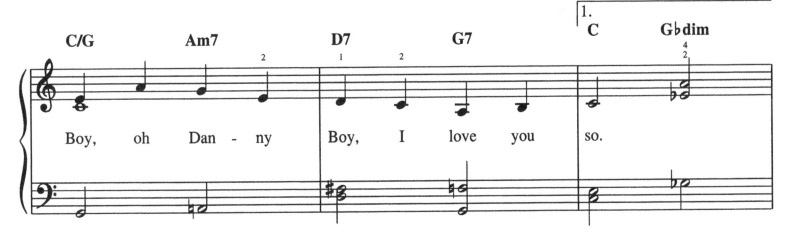

Boy,   oh   Dan - ny   Boy,   I   love   you   so.

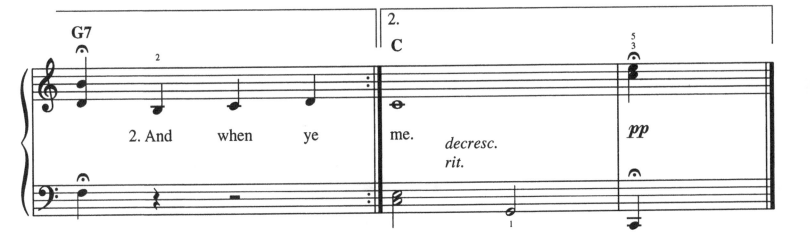

2. And   when   ye   me.   *decresc.*   *rit.*   *pp*

Additional Lyrics

2. And when ye come and all the flowers are dying
If I am dead, as dead I well may be,
You'll come and find the place where I am lying
And kneel and say an Ave there for me.

And I shall hear tho' soft you tread above me
And all my grave will warmer sweeter be;
If you will bend and tell me that you love me,
Then I shall sleep in peace until you come to me.

BELIEVE ME IF ALL THOSE ENDEARING YOUNG CHARMS

With feeling

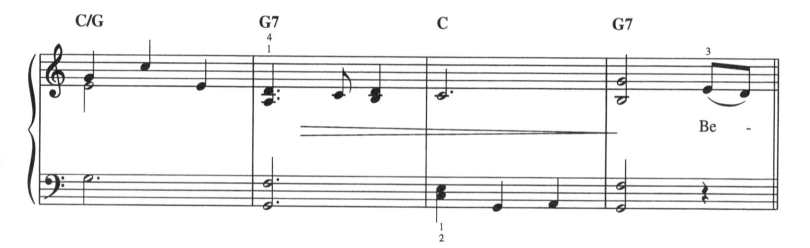

Be -

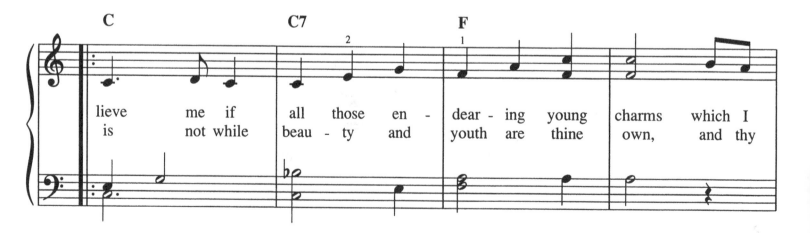

lieve me if all those en - dear - ing young charms which I
is not while beau - ty and youth are thine own, which and thy

9

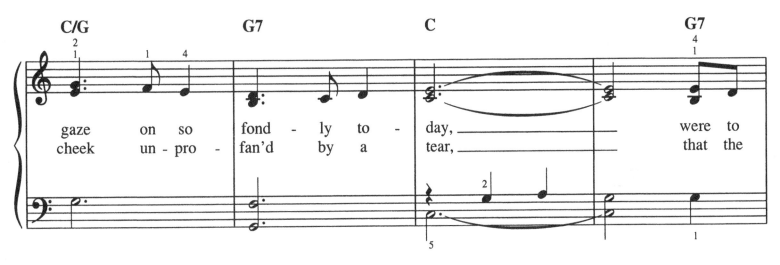

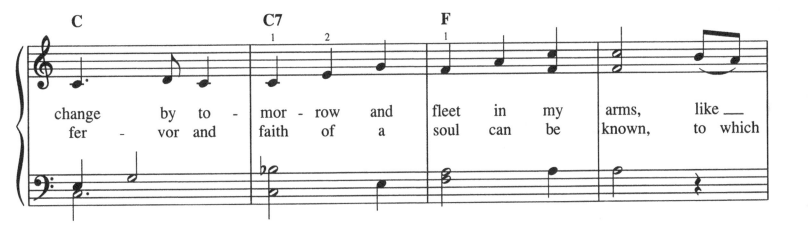

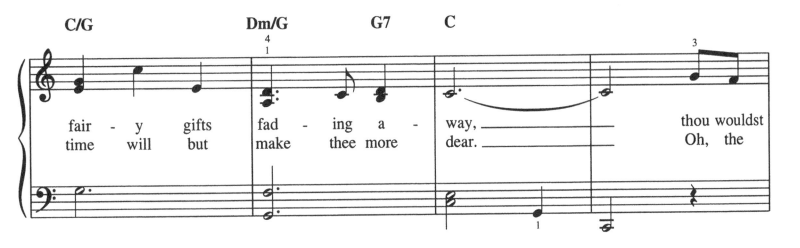

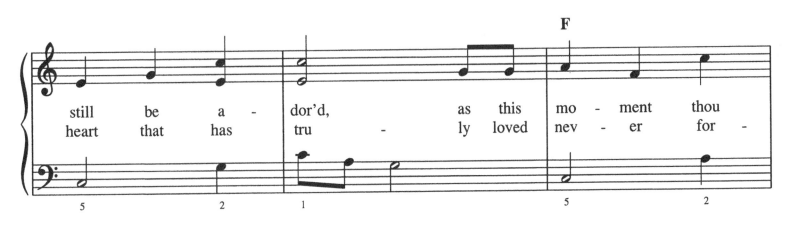

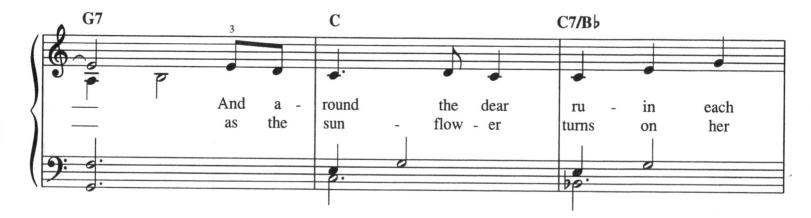

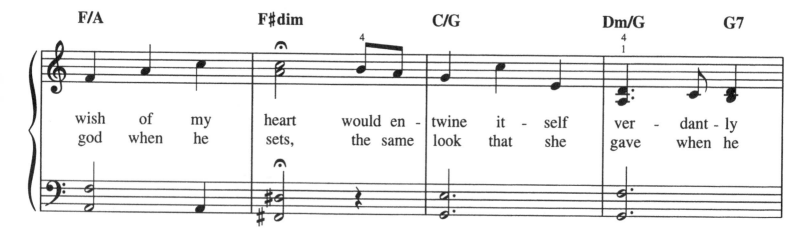

THE GALWAY PIPER

Lively

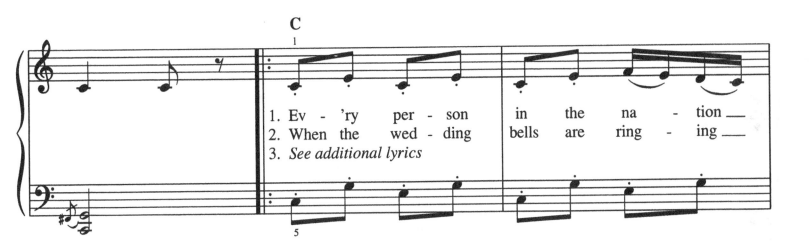

1. Ev - 'ry per - son   in the na - tion ___
2. When the wed - ding   bells are ring - ing ___
3. *See additional lyrics*

or   of   great   or   hum - ble sta - tion ___
his   the   breath   to   lead   the   sing - ing, ___

simile

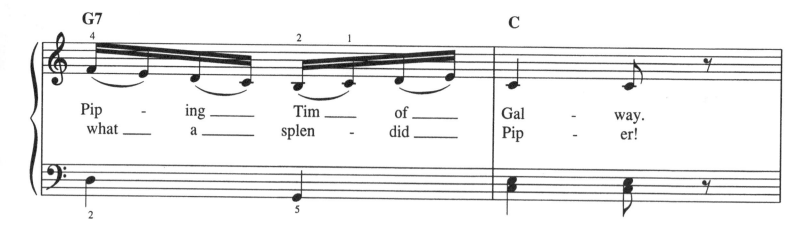

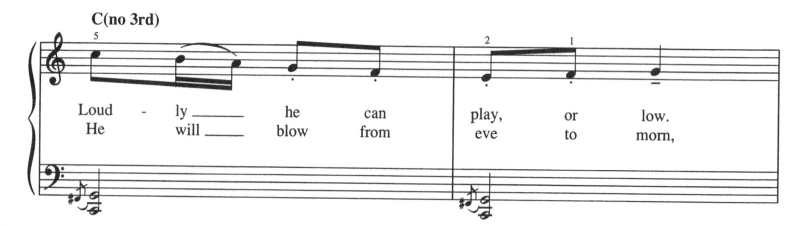

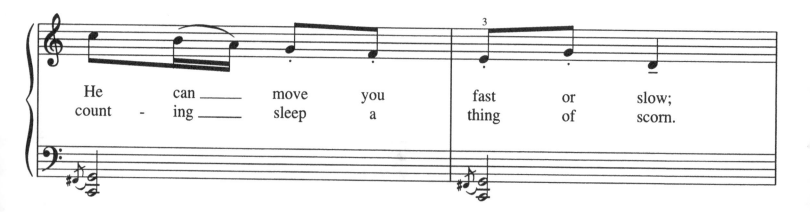

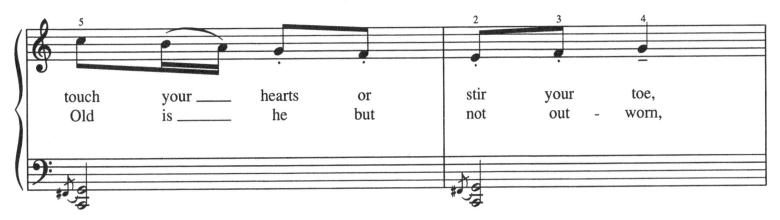

touch your _____ hearts or stir your toe,
Old is _____ he or but not out - worn,

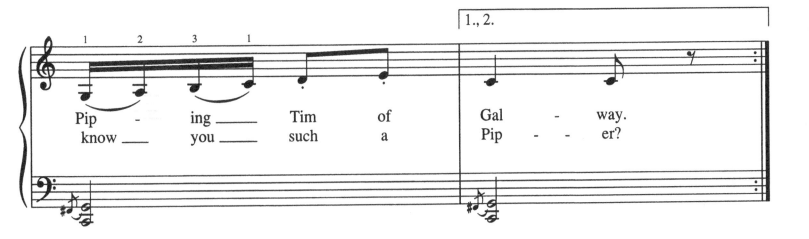

1., 2.

Pip - ing _____ Tim of Gal - way.
know ____ you ____ such a Pip - - er?

3.

Gal - way.

mf — *f*

Additional Lyrics

3. When he walks the highway pealing
   'Round his head the birds come wheeling.
   Tim has carols worth the stealing,
   Piping Tim of Galway.
   Thrush and linnet, finch and lark,
   To each other twitter "Hark!"
   Soon they sing from light to dark
   Pipings learnt in Galway.

GARRYOWEN

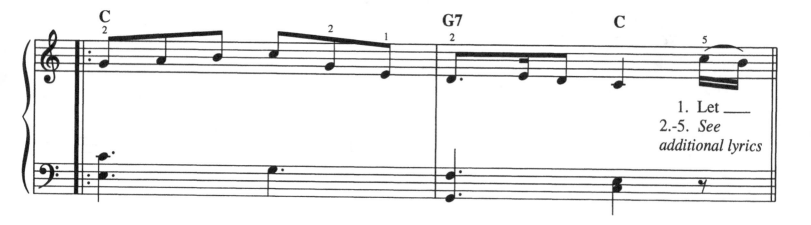

1. Let ____
2.-5. *See*
additional lyrics

Bac - chus' sons ____ be   not ____ dis - mayed,   but ____

join ____ with   me ____ each   jo - vi - al   blade;   come ___

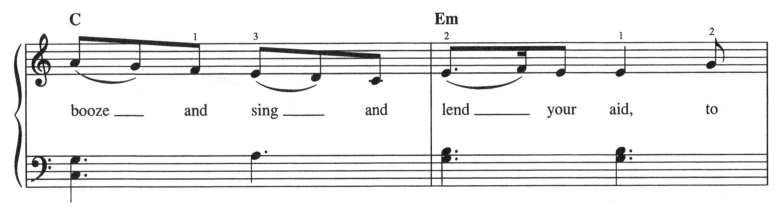

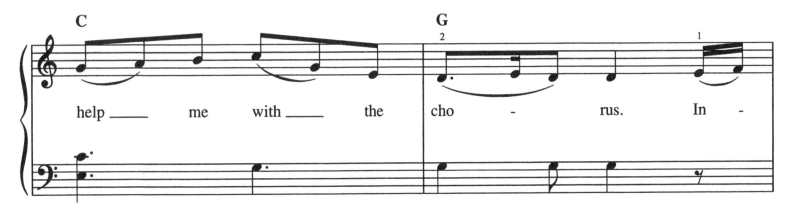

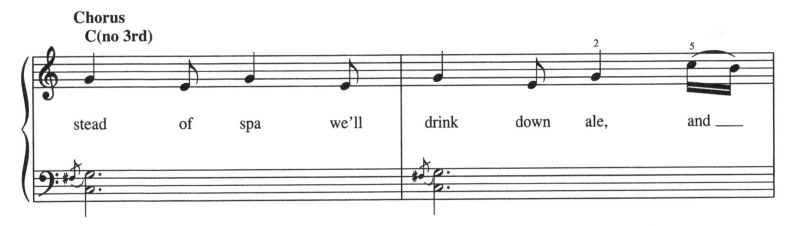

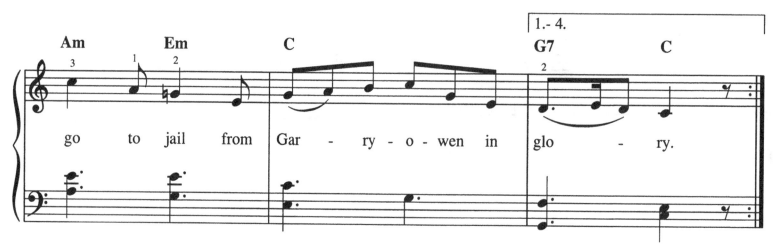

go to jail from Gar - ry - o - wen in glo - ry.

glo - ry.

Additional Lyrics

2. We are the boys that take delight in
Smashing the Limerick lights when lighting.
Through all the streets like sporters fighting,
And tearing all before us.

Chorus:
Instead of spa we'll drink down ale,
And pay the reck'ning on the nail;
No man for debt shall go to jail
From Garryowen in glory.

3. We'll break the windows, we'll break the doors,
The watch knock down by three's and four's;
Then let the doctors work their cures,
And tinker up our bruises.
To Chorus:

4. We'll beat the bailiffs out of fun,
We'll make the mayors and sheriffs run;
We are the boys no man dares dun,
If he regards a whole skin.
To Chorus:

5. Our hearts so stout have got us fame,
For soon 'tis known from whence we came;
Where'er we go they dread the name
Of Garryowen in glory.
To Chorus:

THE GIRL I LEFT BEHIND ME

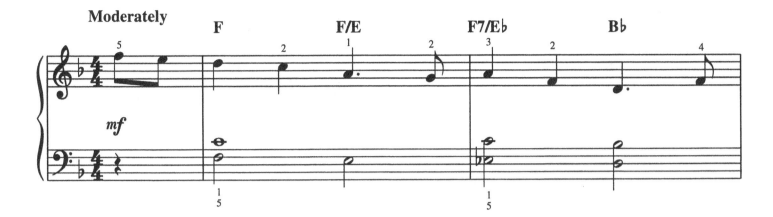

1. The ____

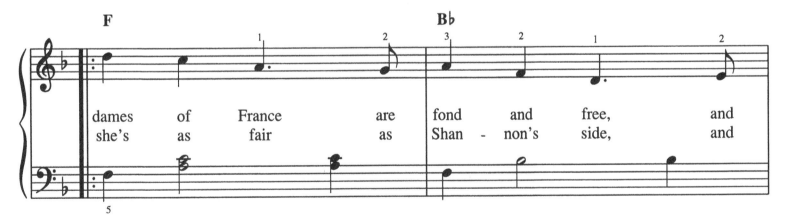

dames   of   France   are   fond   and   free,   and
she's   as   fair   as   Shan - non's   side,   and

Flem - ish   lips ____ are ____   will - ing,   and ____
pur - er   than ____ its ____   wa - ter.   But ____

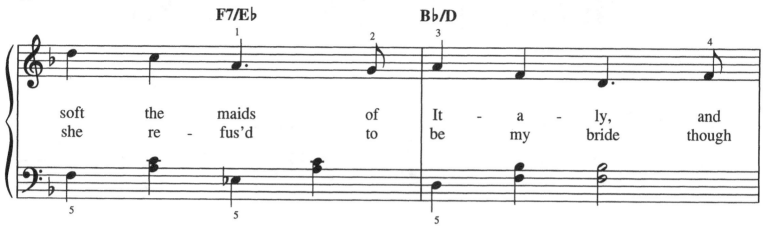

soft the maids of It - a - ly, and
she re - fus'd to be my bride and though

Span - ish eyes are ___ thrill - ing. Still ___ though I bask be -
many a year I ___ sought ___ her. Yet ___ since to France I

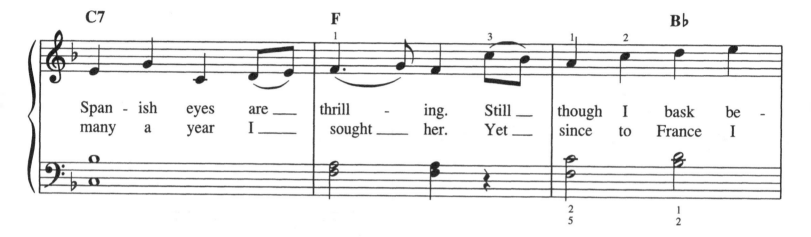

neath their smile, their charms ___ fail to
sail'd a - way, her let - ters oft re -

bind me, and my heart falls back to
mind me, that I prom - is'd nev - er

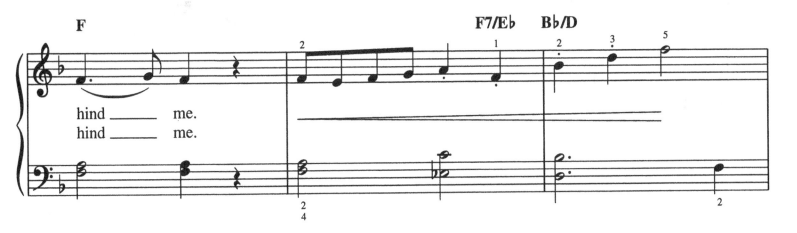

Additional Lyrics

3. She says "My own dear love, come home,
   my friends are rich and many;
   Or else abroad with you I'll roam,
   a soldier stout as any.
   If you'll not come, nor let me go,
   I'll think you have resigned me."
   My heart nigh broke when I answered "No"
   to the girl I left behind me.

4. For never shall my true love brave
   a life of war and toiling,
   And never as a skulking slave
   I'll tread my native soil on.
   But were it free or to be freed,
   the battle's close would find me,
   To Ireland bound, nor message need
   from the girl I left behind me.

THE HARP THAT ONCE THRO' TARA'S HALLS

Moderately slow

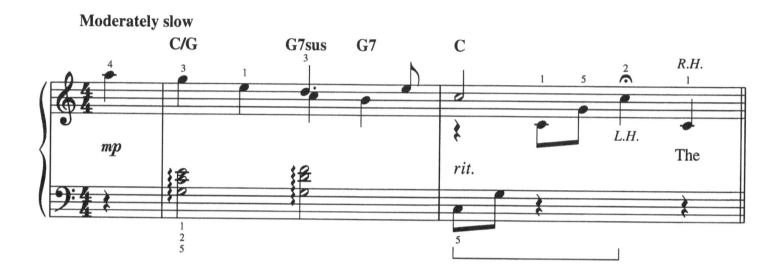

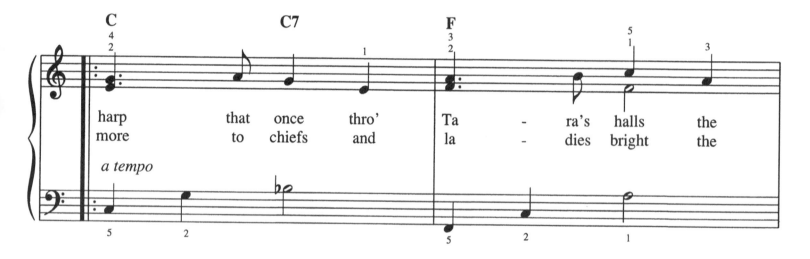

harp   that once thro'   Ta - ra's halls   the
more   to chiefs and   la - dies bright   the

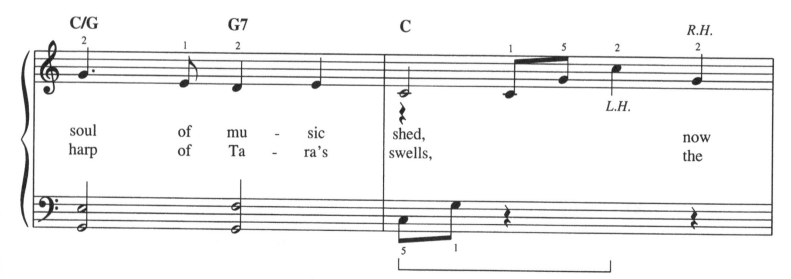

soul   of mu - sic   shed,   now
harp   of Ta - ra's   swells,   the

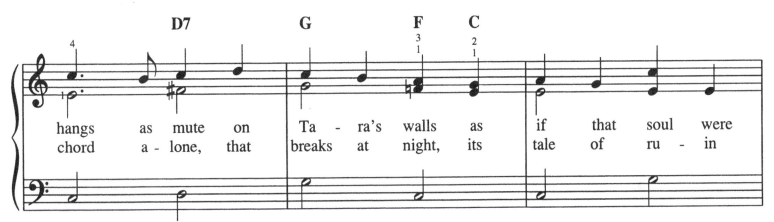

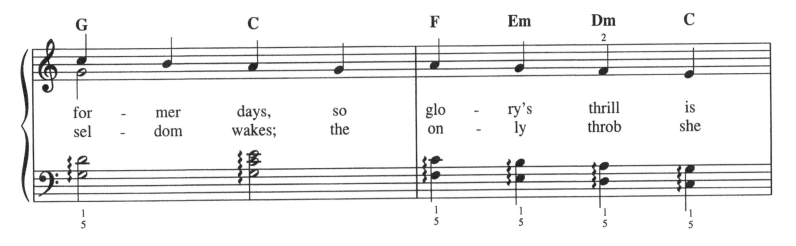

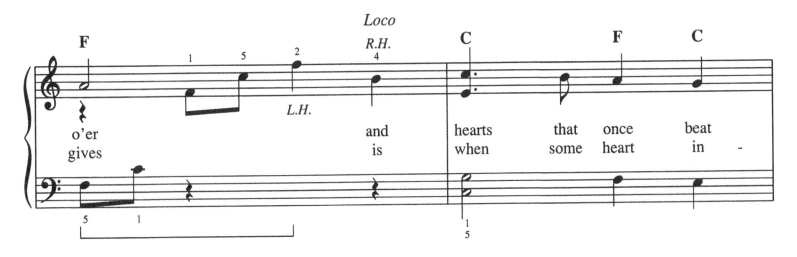

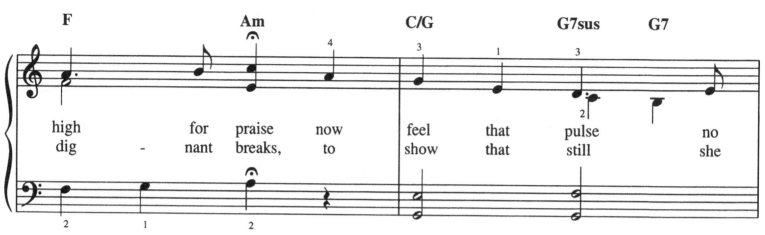

high   for praise now feel that pulse   no
dig - nant breaks, to show that still she

1. C

more.

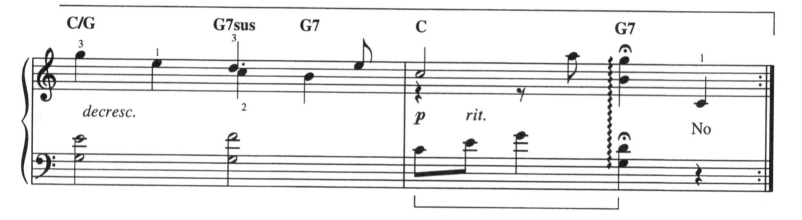

C/G   **G7sus** **G7** **C**   **G7**

decresc.   *p rit.*   No

2.

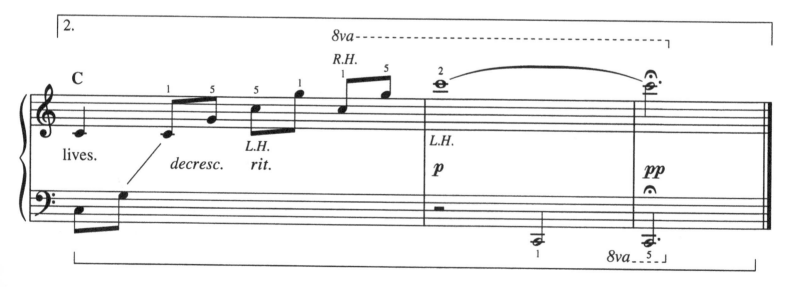

C

lives. *decresc. rit.*

HAS SORROW THY YOUNG DAYS SHADED?

Moderately slow

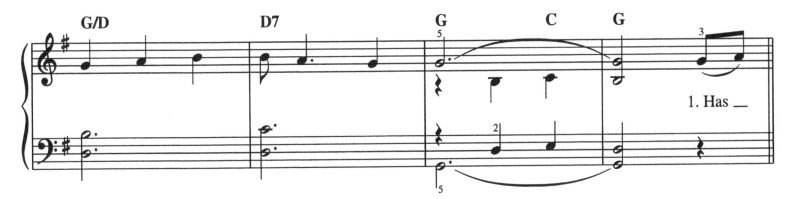

1. Has ___

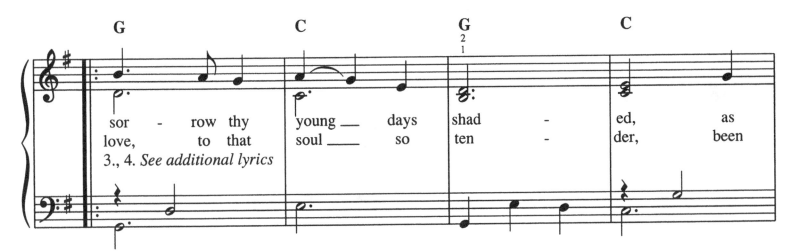

sor - row thy young ___ days shad - ed, as
love, to that soul ___ so ten - der, been
3., 4. *See additional lyrics*

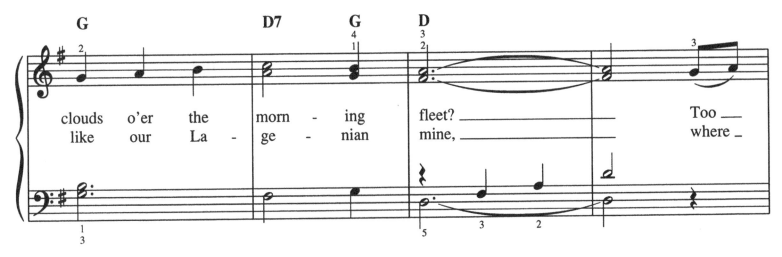

clouds o'er the morn - ing fleet? ___ Too ___
like our La - ge - nian mine, ___ where ___

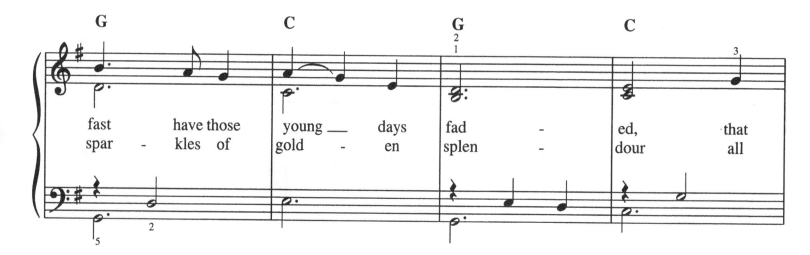

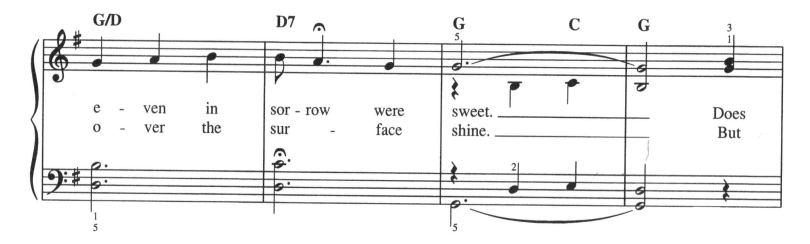

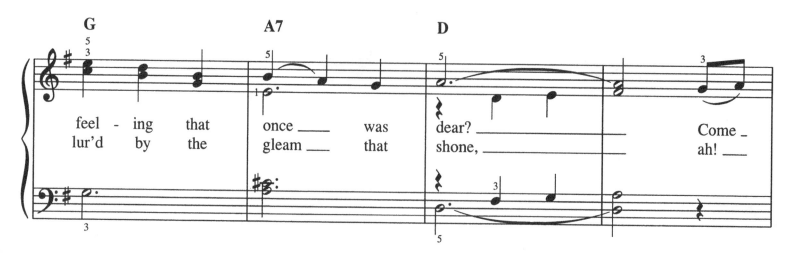

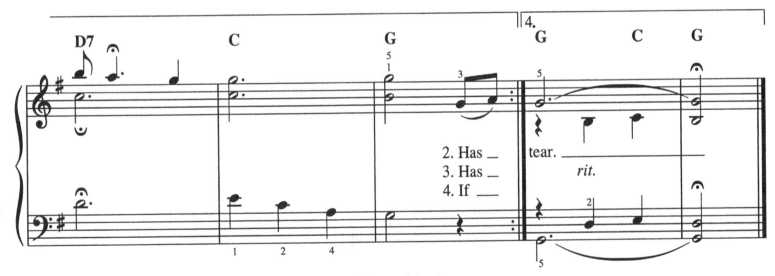

Additional Lyrics

3. Has hope, like the bird in the story, that flitted from tree to tree,
   With the talisman's glittering glory, has hope been that bird to thee?
   On branch after branch alighting, the gem did she still display,
   And, when nearest and most inviting, then waft the fair gem away.

4. If thus the sweet hours have fleeted, when sorrow herself look'd bright;
   If thus the fond hope has cheated, that led thee along so light;
   If thus the unkind world wither, each feeling that once was dear;
   Come, child of misfortune! Come hither, I'll weep with thee, tear for tear.

HARRIGAN

With a lilt (♪♪ = ♩♪)

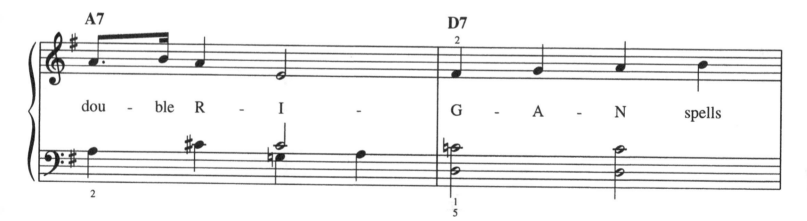

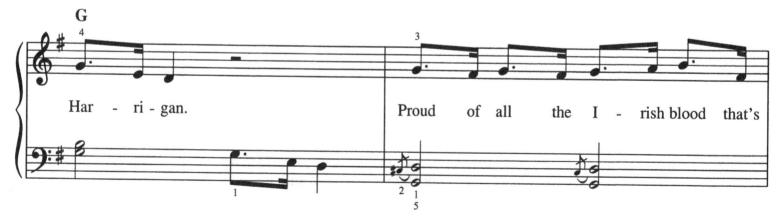

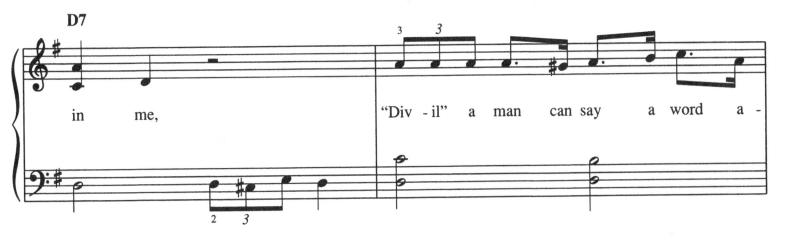

in me,　　　　　　"Div-il" a man can say　a word a-

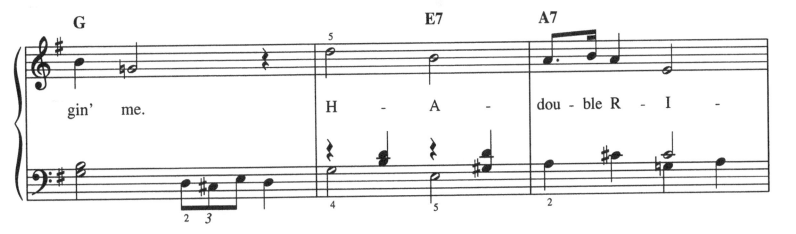

gin' me.　　　H - A -　dou-ble R - I -

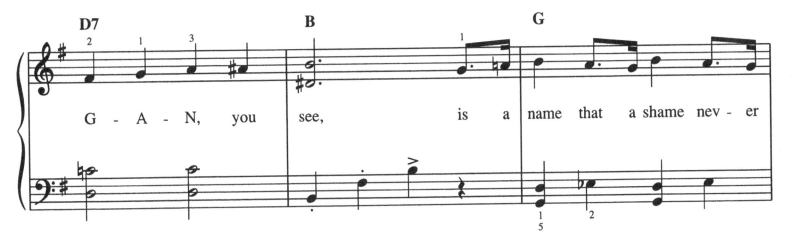

G - A - N, you　see,　　is a name that a shame nev-er

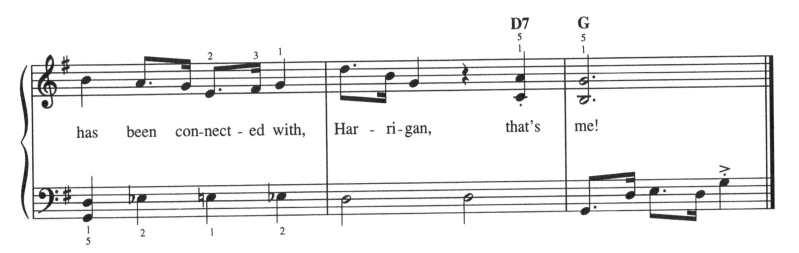

has　been con-nect-ed with,　Har-ri-gan,　that's　me!

HAS ANYBODY HERE SEEN KELLY?

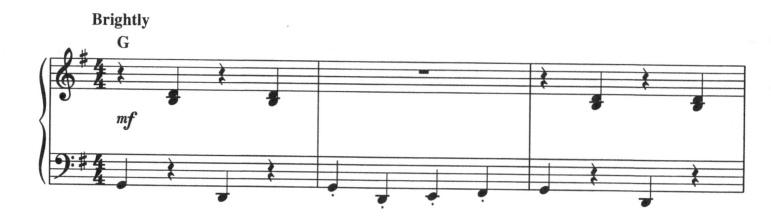

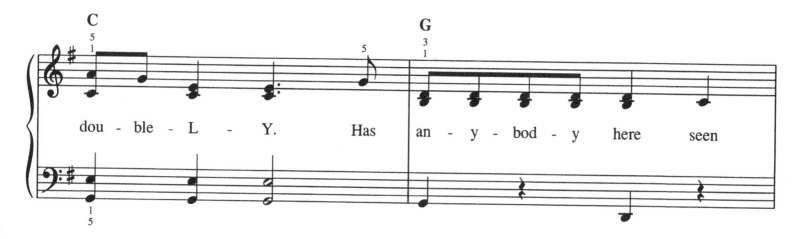

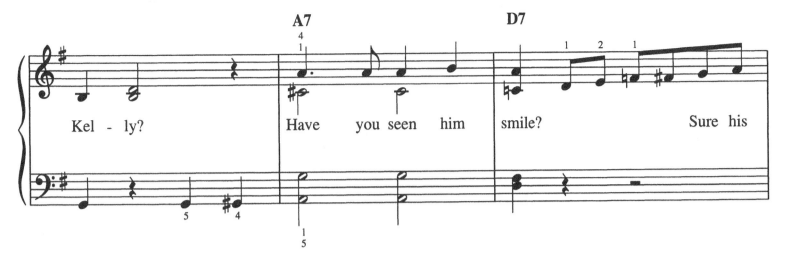

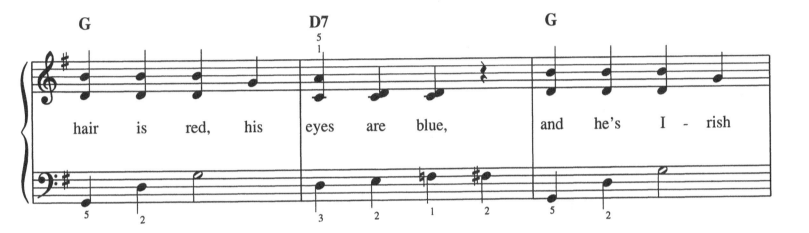

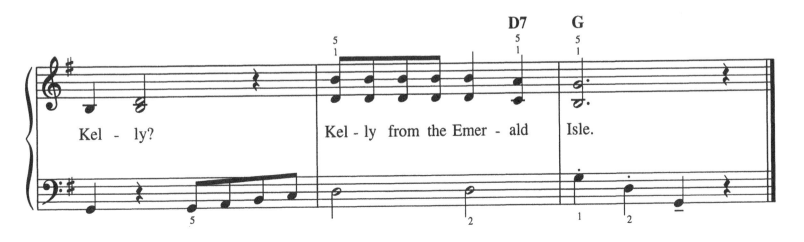

IF I KNOCK THE "L" OUT OF KELLY

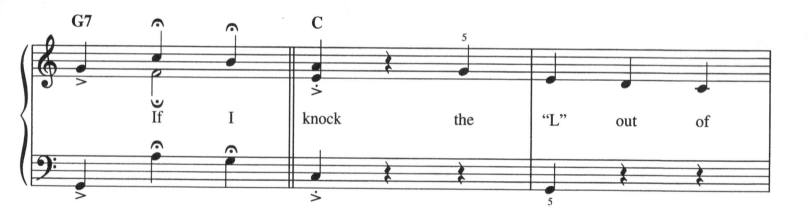

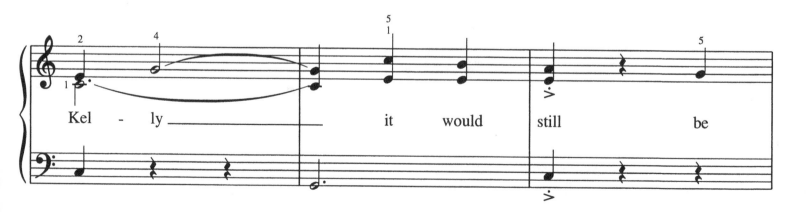

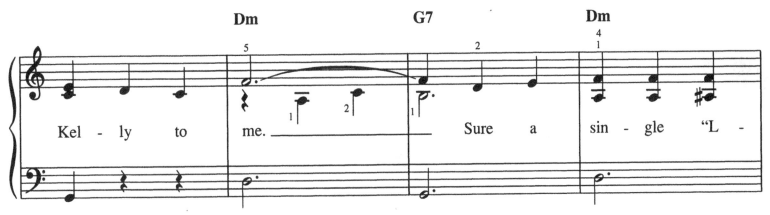

Kel - ly to me. _____ Sure a sin - gle "L -

Y" or a dou - ble "L - Y" should

look just the same to an I - rish - man's

eye. Knock off an "L" from Kil - lar - ney, _____

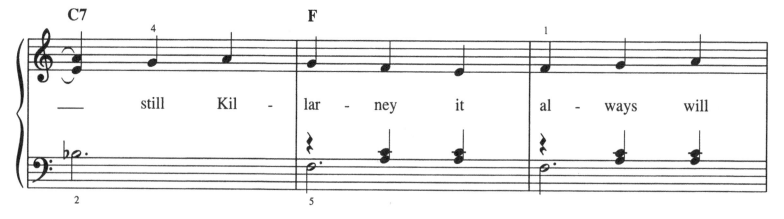

C7   **F**

still Kil - lar - ney it al - ways will

F#dim   **C**

be. But if I knock the

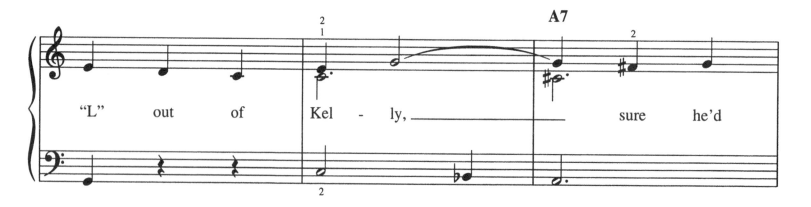

A7

"L" out of Kel - ly, sure he'd

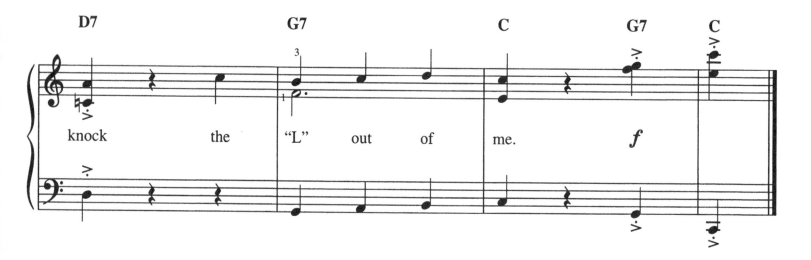

D7   **G7**   **C**   **G7**   **C**

knock the "L" out of me. *f*

I'LL TAKE YOU HOME AGAIN, KATHLEEN

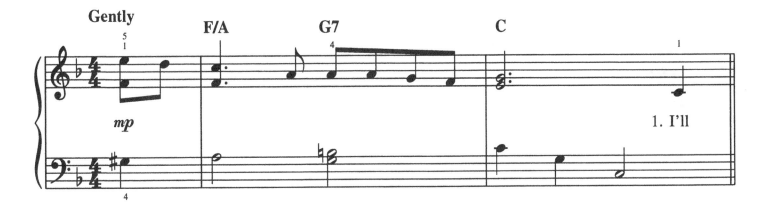

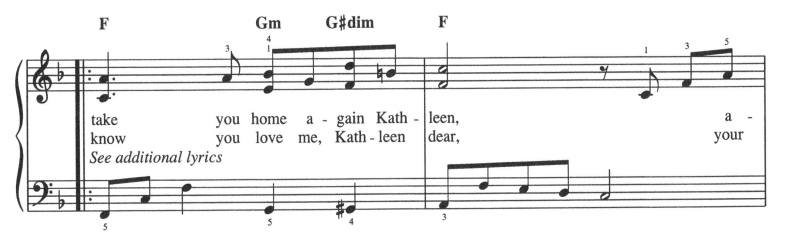

take   you home a - gain Kath - leen,   a -
know   you love me, Kath - leen dear,   your
See additional lyrics

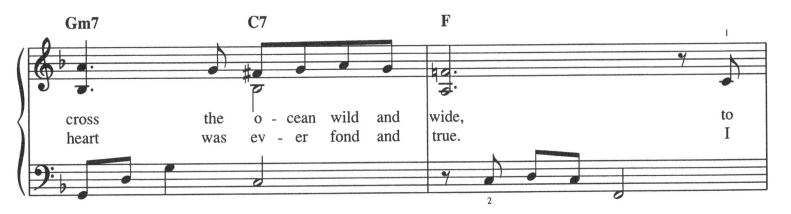

cross   the o - cean wild and wide,   to
heart   was ev - er fond and true.   I

where   your heart has ev - er been,   since that
al   - ways feel when you are near

34

first   you were my bon - nie   bride.   The
life   holds noth - ing dear but   you.   The

ros -   es   all   have left your   cheek;   I've
smiles   that once you gave to   me,   I

watched   them fade a - way and   die.   Your voice   is sad when-e'er you
scarce - ly   ev - er see them   now.   The man - y, man - y times I

speak,   and   tears   be - dim your lov - ing   eye. }
see   a   dark - 'ning shad - ow on your   brow. }
                                                   Oh,

CHORUS

I will take you back, Kath- leen, to where your heart will feel no

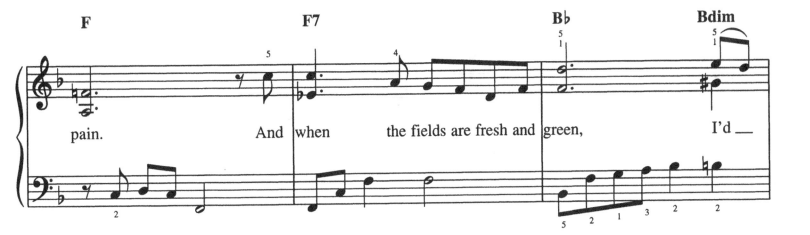

pain. And when the fields are fresh and green, I'd __

take you home a - gain, Kath - leen.

{ 2. I
{ 3. To

leen. _____

rit.

Additional Lyrics

3. To that dear home beyond the sea,
   My Kathleen shall again return.
   And when thy old friends welcome thee,
   Thy loving heart will cease to yearn.
   Where laughs the little silver stream,
   Beside your mother's humble cot,
   And brightest rays of sunshine gleam,
   There all your grief will be forgot.

To Chorus:

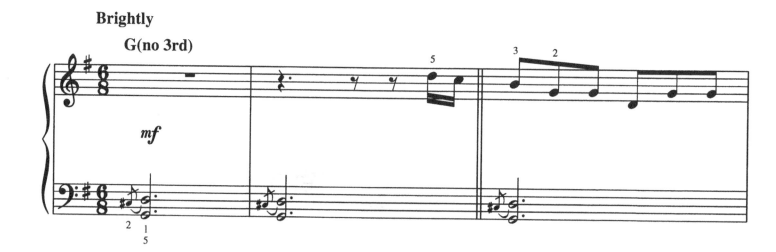

THE IRISH WASHERWOMAN

Brightly

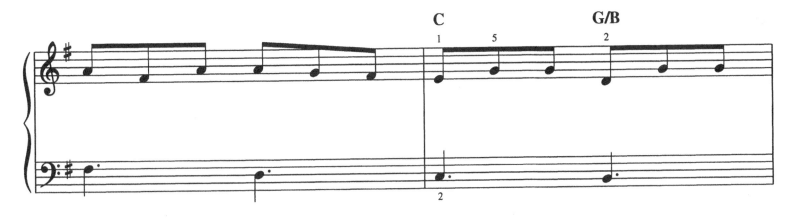

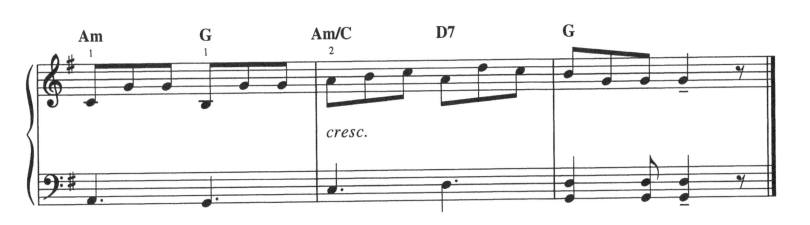

KATHLEEN MAVOURNEEN

With expression

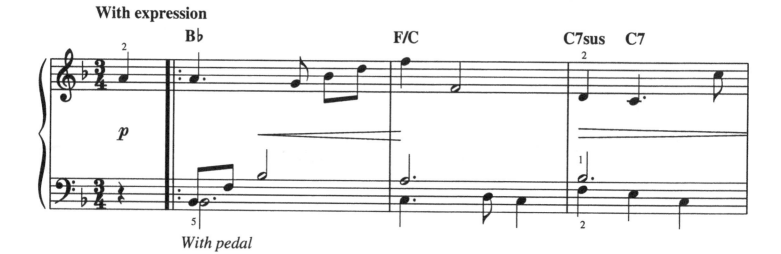

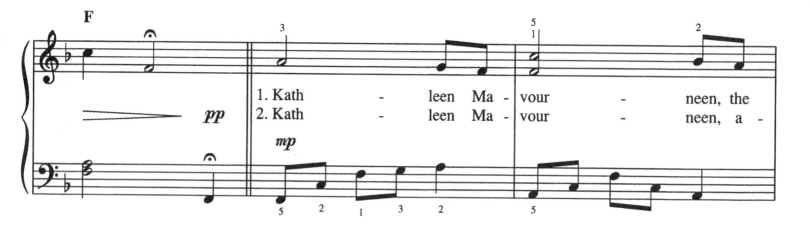

1. Kath - leen Ma - vour - neen, the
2. Kath - leen Ma - vour - neen, a -

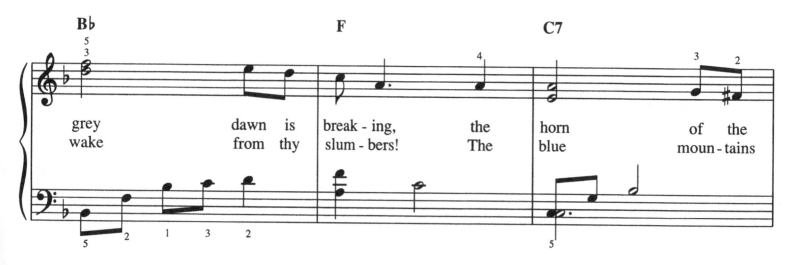

grey   dawn is break - ing,   the horn   of the
wake   from thy slum - bers!   The blue   moun - tains

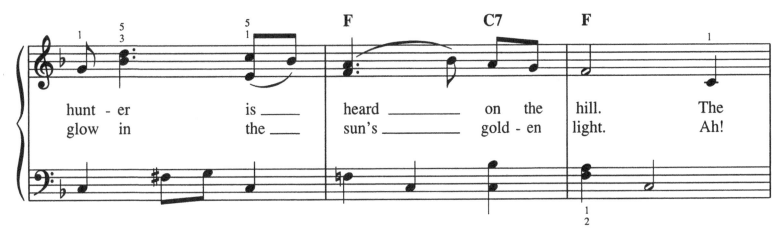

hunt - er is _____ heard _____ on the hill. The
glow in the _____ sun's _____ gold - en light. Ah!

lark from her light wing the bright _____ dew is
where is the light spell that once hung _____ on my

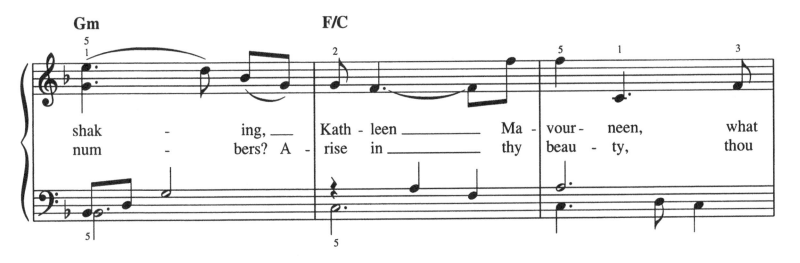

shak - ing, _____ Kath - leen _____ Ma - vour - neen, what
num - bers? A - rise in _____ thy beau - ty, thou

slum - b'ring still! Oh, hast thou for -
star of my night! Ma - vour - neen, Ma -

40

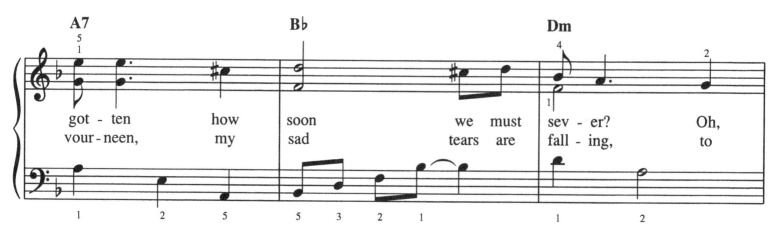

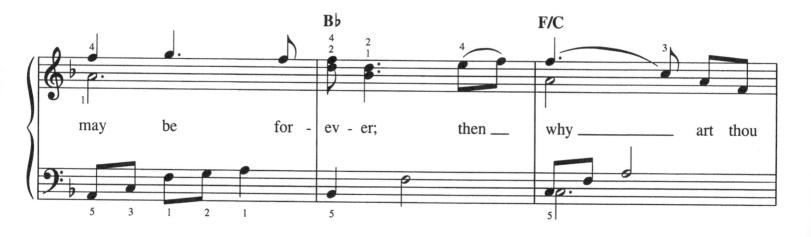

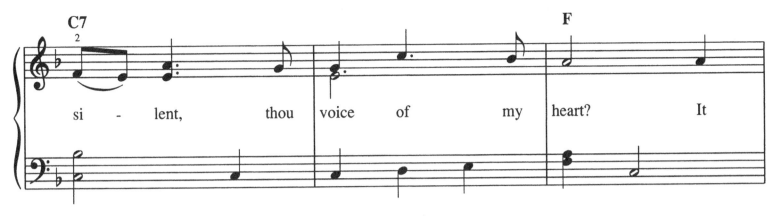

si - lent, thou voice of my heart? It

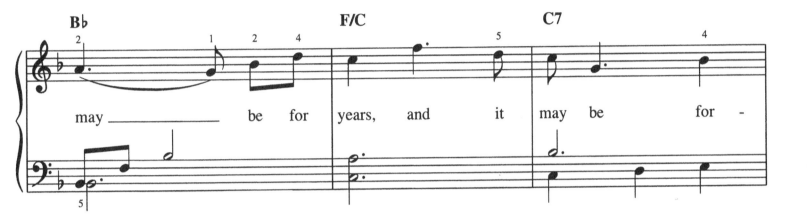

may _____ be for years, and it may be for -

ev - er; then why _____ are thou si - lent,

Kath - leen Ma - vour - neen? vour - neen?

1. F

2. F

rit.

THE KERRY DANCE

Brightly

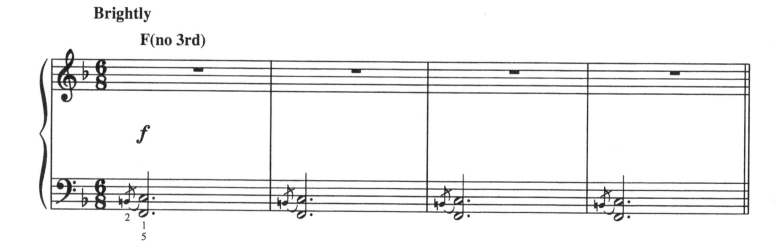

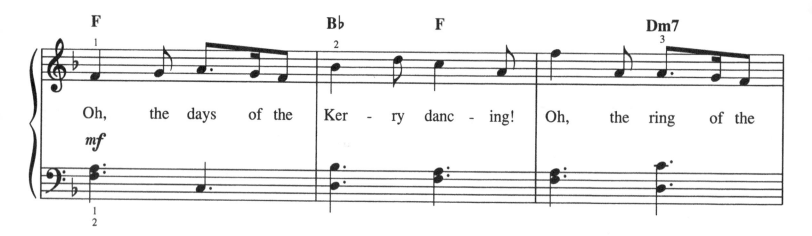

Oh, the days of the Ker-ry danc-ing! Oh, the ring of the

pi - - per's tune! Oh, for one of those

hours of glad - ness, gone a - las! like our youth, too soon!

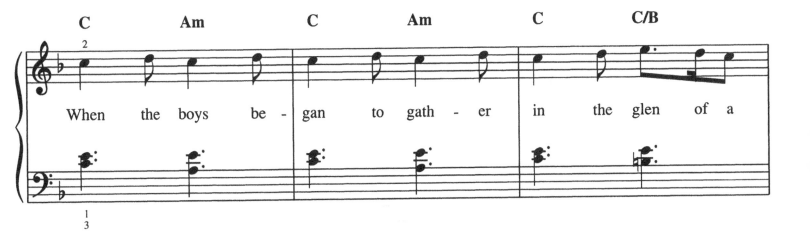

When the boys be - gan to gath - er in the glen of a

sum - mer night, and the Ker - ry pi - per's tun - ing

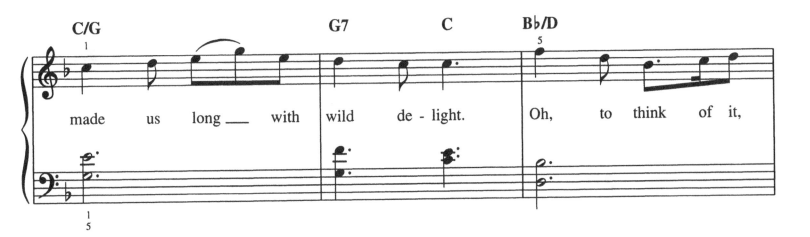

made us long ___ with wild de - light. Oh, to think of it,

44

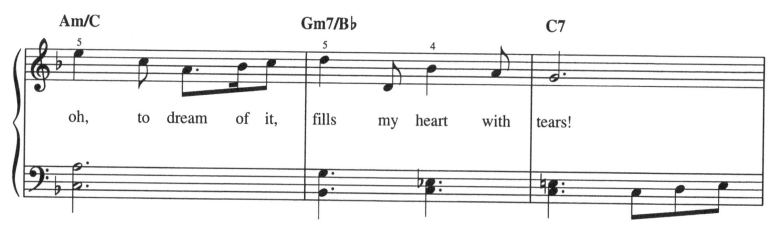

oh, to dream of it, fills my heart with tears!

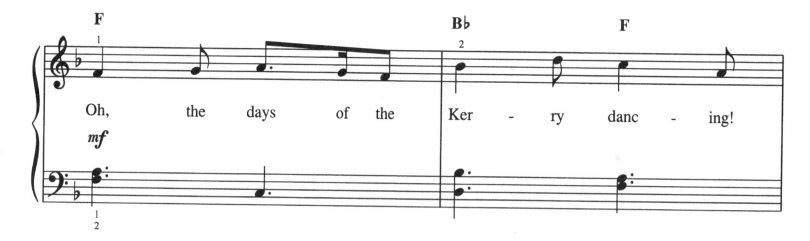

Oh, the days of the Ker - ry danc - ing!

mf

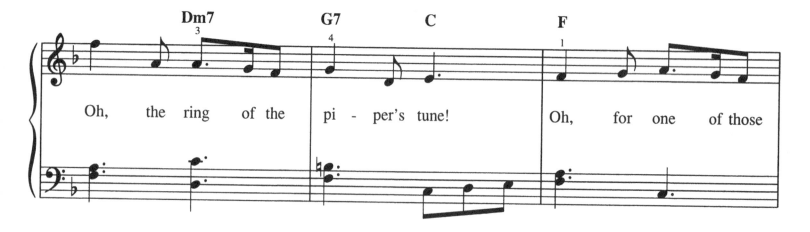

Oh, the ring of the pi - per's tune! Oh, for one of those

hours of glad - ness, gone a - las! like our youth, too soon!

KILLARNEY

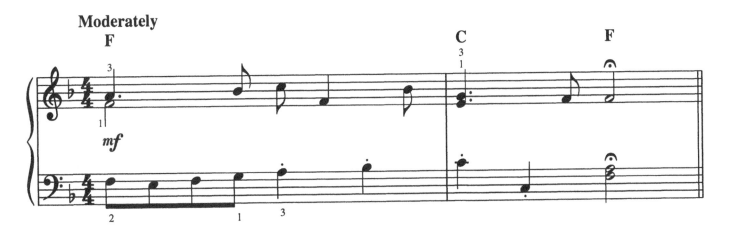

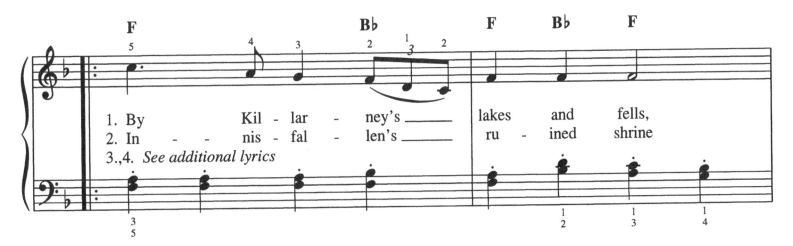

1. By Kil - lar - ney's _____ lakes and fells,
2. In - - nis - fal - len's _____ ru - ined shrine

3.,4. *See additional lyrics*

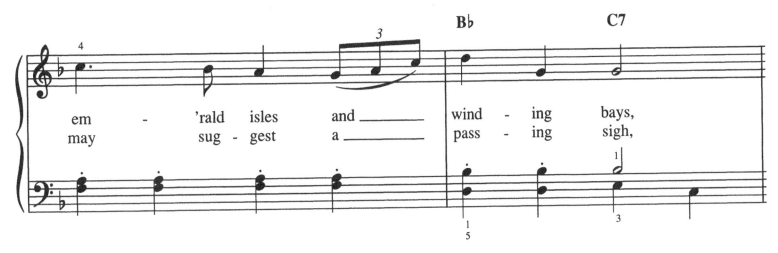

em - 'rald isles and _____ wind - ing bays,
may sug - gest a _____ pass - ing sigh,

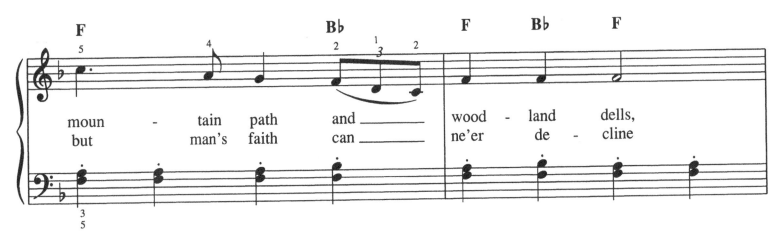

moun - tain path and _____ wood - land dells,
but man's faith can _____ ne'er de - cline

46

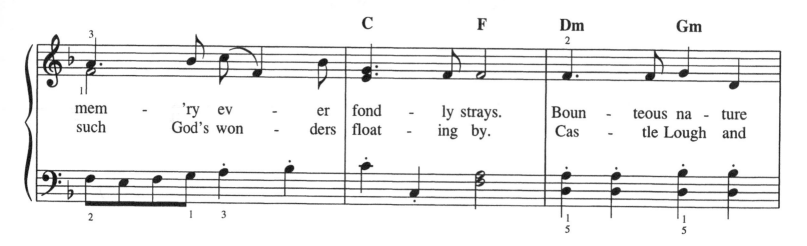

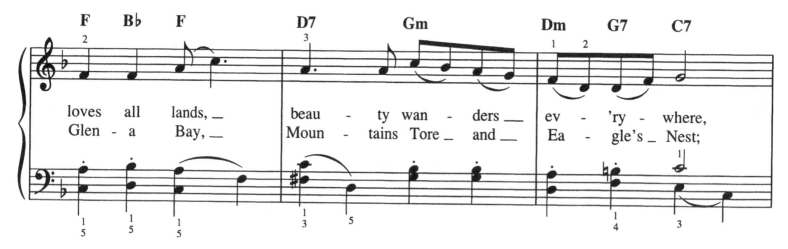

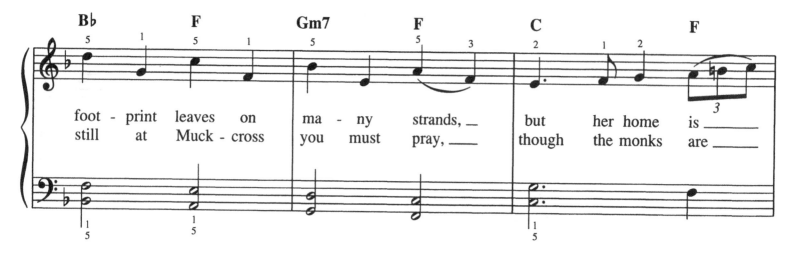

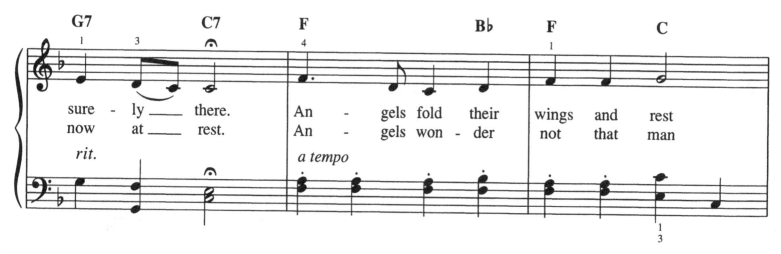

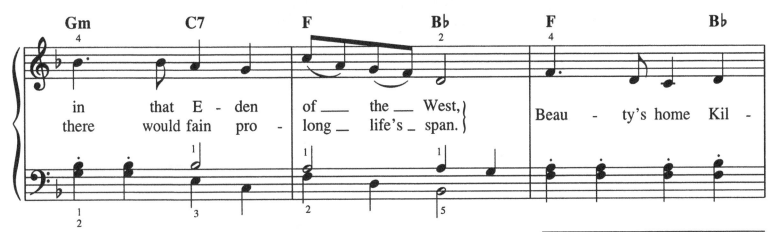

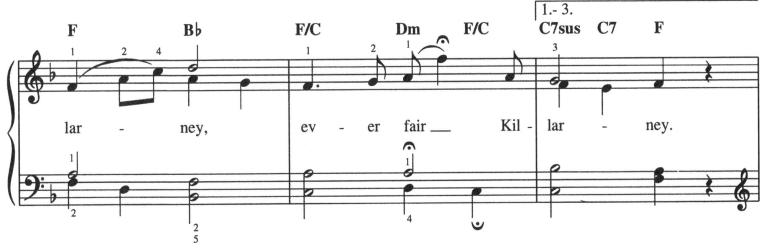

Additional Lyrics

3. No place else can charm the eye with such bright and varied tints;
   Ev'ry rock that you pass by, verdure 'broider or besprints.
   Virgin there the green grass grows; ev'ry morn springs natal day;
   Bright-hued berries daff the snows, smiling winter's frowns away.
   Angels often pausing there doubt if Eden were more fair;
   Beauty's home Killarney, ever fair Killarney.

4. Music there for echo dwells, makes each sound a harmony;
   Many voiced the chorus swells, till it faints in ecstacy.
   With the charmful tints below, seems the Heav'n above to vie;
   All rich colors that we know tinge the cloud-wreaths in that sky.
   Wings of angels so might shine, glancing back soft light divine;
   Beauty's home Killarney, ever fair Killarney.

KITTY OF COLERAINE

Moderately fast

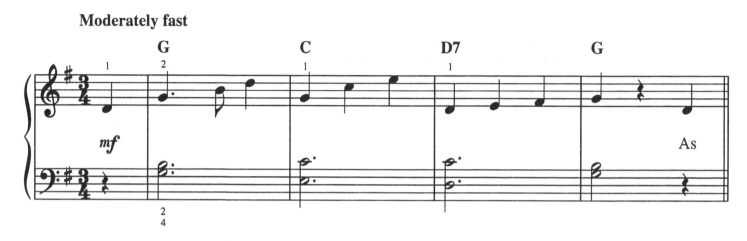

mf

As

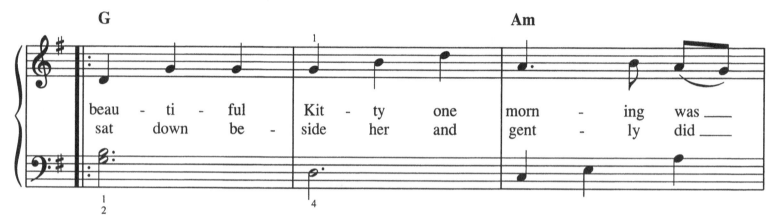

beau - ti - ful / sat down be -

Kit - ty one / side her and

morn - ing was ___ / gent - ly did ___

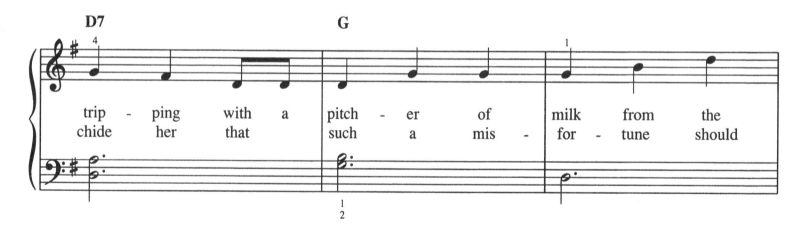

trip - ping with a / chide her with that

pitch - er of / such a mis -

milk from the / for - tune the should

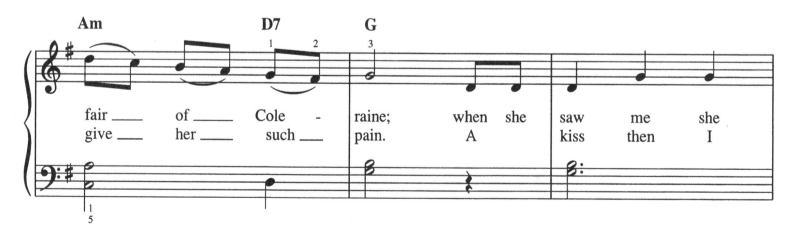

fair ___ of ___ Cole - / give ___ her ___ such ___

raine; when she / pain. A

saw me she / kiss me then I

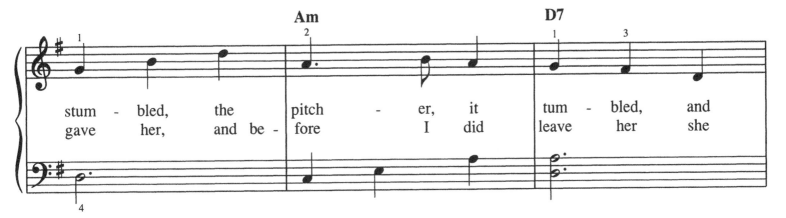

Am · D7

stum - bled, the pitch - er, it tum - bled, and
gave her, and be - fore I did leave her and she

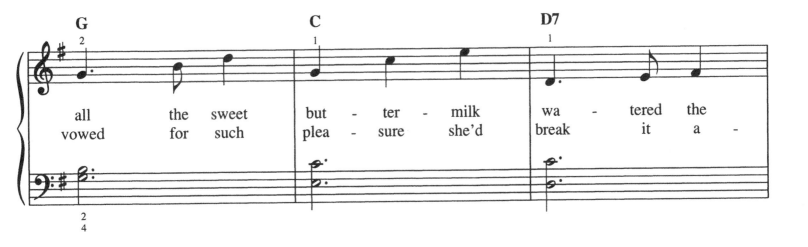

G · C · D7

all the sweet but - ter - milk wa - tered the
vowed for such plea - sure she'd break it a -

G · D

plain. "Oh, ___ what shall I do now? 'Twas
gain. 'Twas ___ hay - mak - ing sea - son, I

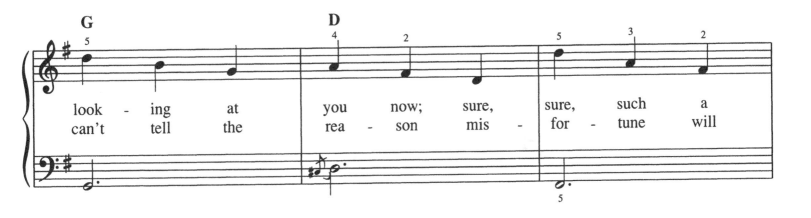

G · D

look - ing at you now; sure, sure, such a
can't tell at the rea - son mis - for - tune will

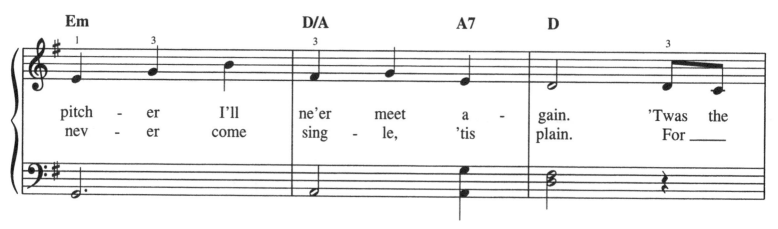

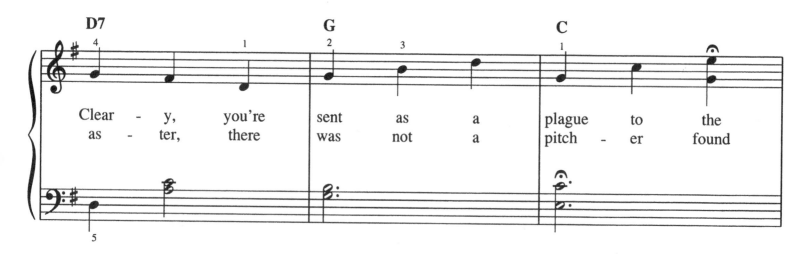

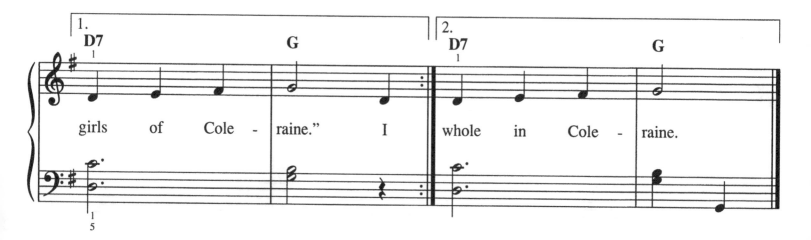

McNAMARA'S BAND

1. Oh! me name is Mc - Na - mar - a, I'm the
2. Right now we are re - hears - in' for a

lead - er of the band. ___ Al - though we're few in
ver - y swell af - fair, ___ the an - nual cel - e -

num - bers, we're the fin - est in the land. We
bra - tion, all the gen - try will be there. When

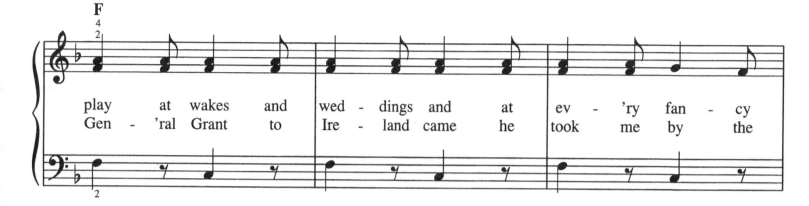

play at wakes and wed - dings and at ev - 'ry fan - cy
Gen - 'ral Grant to Ire - land came he took me by the

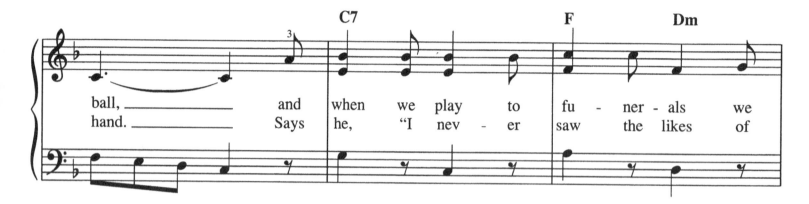

ball, _____ and when we play to fu - ner - als we
hand. _____ Says he, "I nev - er saw the likes of

play the March from Saul. }
Mc - Na - mar - a's Band. } Oh! the drums go bang and the

cym - bals clang, and the horns they blaze a - way. _____ Mc -

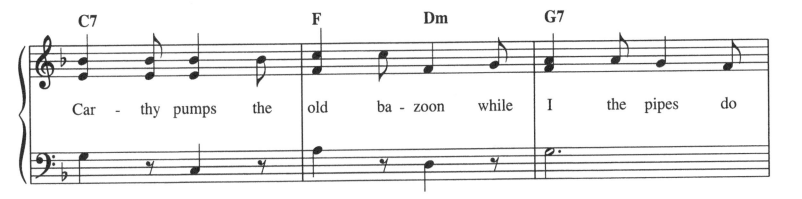

Car - thy pumps the old ba - zoon while I the pipes do

play. And Hen - nes - sey Ten - nes - sey toot - les the flute, and the

mu - sic is some - thin' grand. _____ A cred - it to old

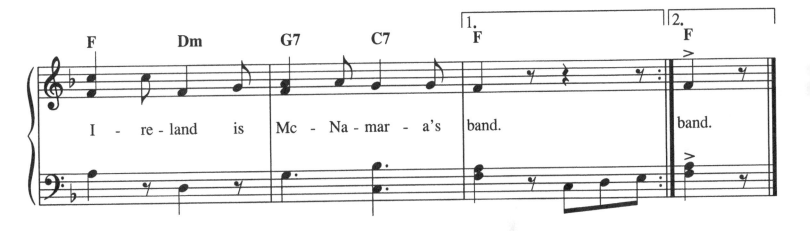

I - re - land is Mc - Na - mar - a's band. band.

A LITTLE BIT OF HEAVEN
(Shure They Call It Ireland)

With expression

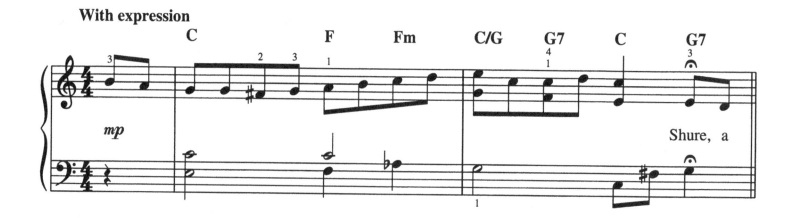

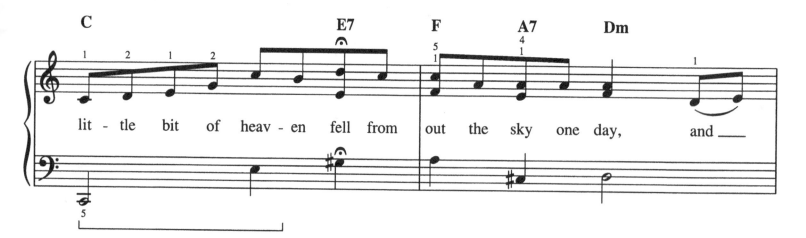

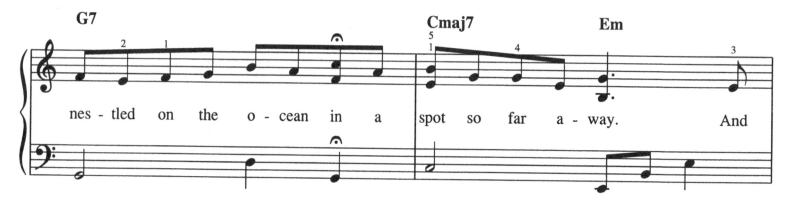

said sup - pose we leave it, for it looks so peace - ful there. So they

sprink - led it with star - dust just to make the sham - rocks grow; 'tis the

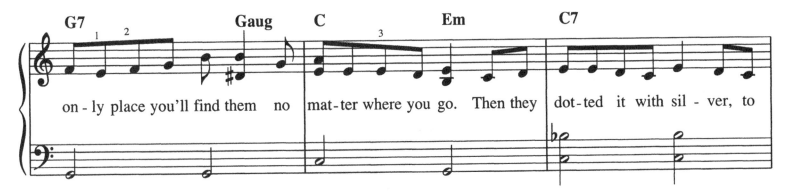

on - ly place you'll find them no mat - ter where you go. Then they dot - ted it with sil - ver, to

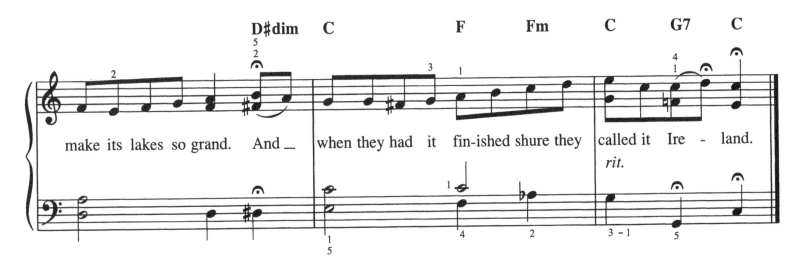

make its lakes so grand. And __ when they had it fin - ished shure they called it Ire - land.

rit.

THE MINSTREL BOY

With expression

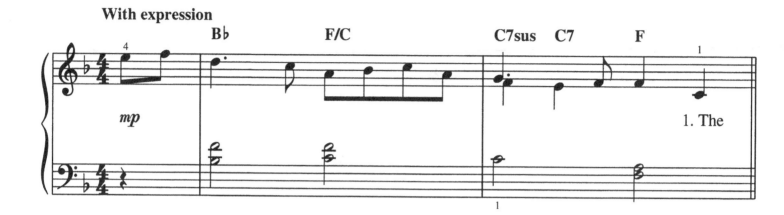

1. The

min - strel boy ____ to the war is gone, in the
min - strel fell ____ but the foe - man's chain could not

ranks of death ____ you'll find ____ him. His
bring his proud ____ soul un - der. The

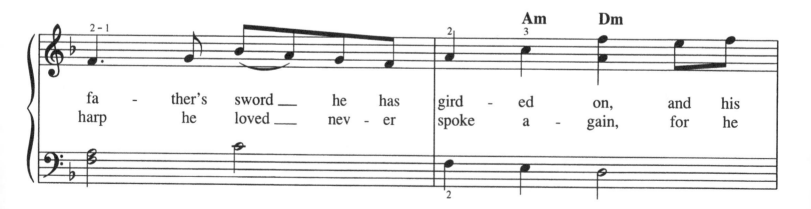

fa - ther's sword ____ he has gird - ed on, and his
harp he loved ____ nev - er spoke a - gain, for he

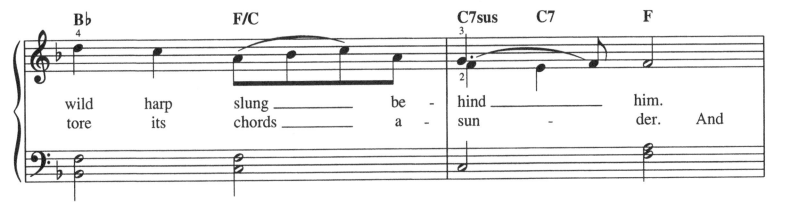

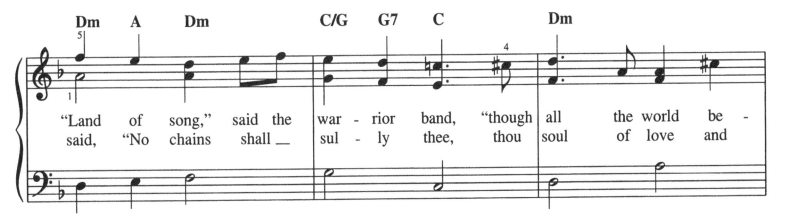

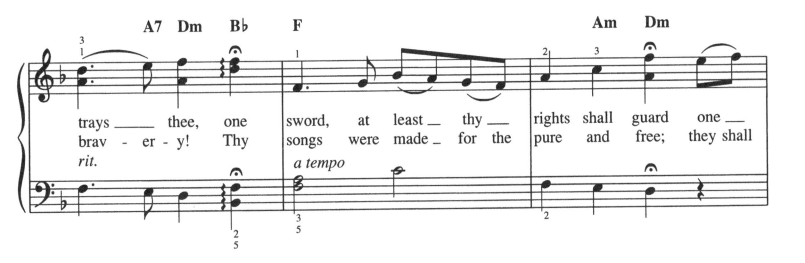

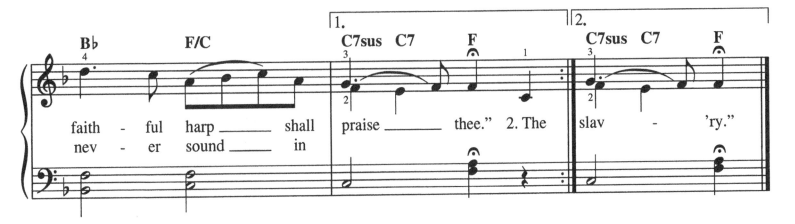

MOLLY MALONE
(Cockles and Mussels)

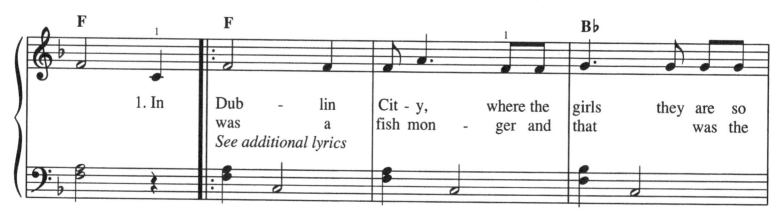

1. In Dub - lin Cit - y, where the girls they are so
was a fish mon - ger and that they was the
See additional lyrics

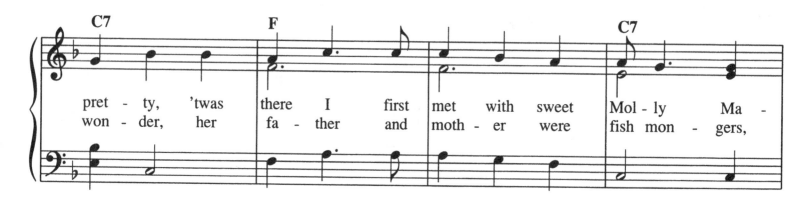

pret - ty, 'twas there I first met with sweet Mol - ly Ma -
won - der, her fa - ther and moth - er were fish mon - gers,

lone. She drove a wheel - bar - row thro' streets broad and
too. They drove wheel - bar - rows thro' streets broad and

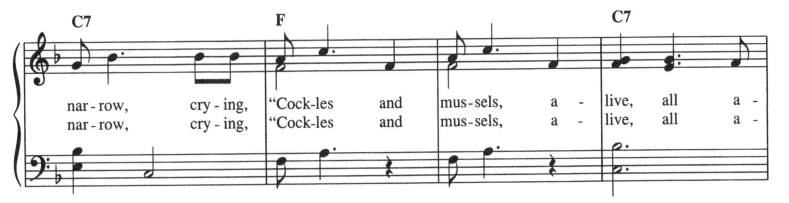

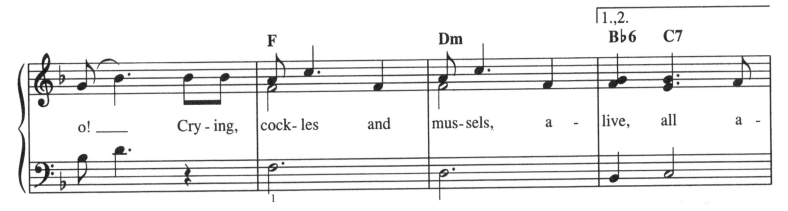

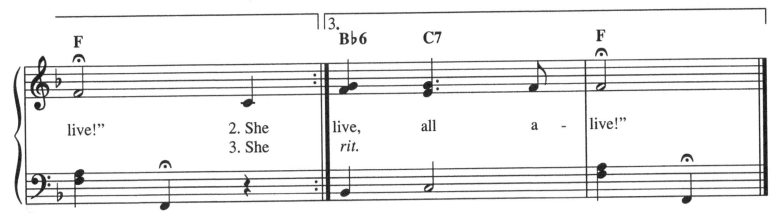

Additional Lyrics

3. She died of a faver, and nothing could save her,
   And that was the end of sweet Molly Malone.
   But her ghost drives a barrow thro' streets broad and narrow,
   Crying, "Cockles and mussels, alive, all alive!"

   To Chorus

MY WILD IRISH ROSE

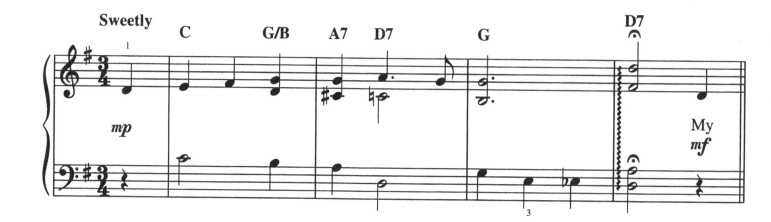

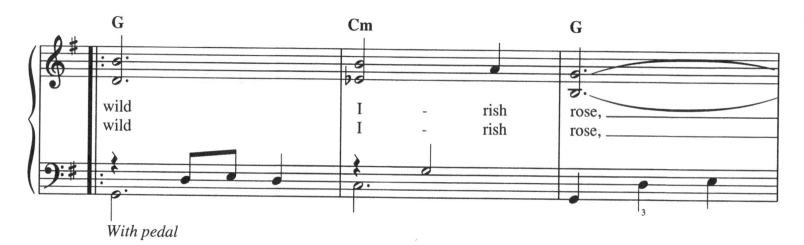

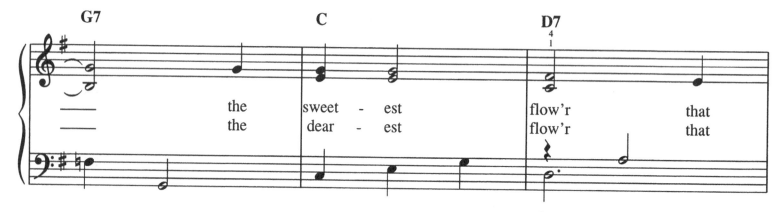

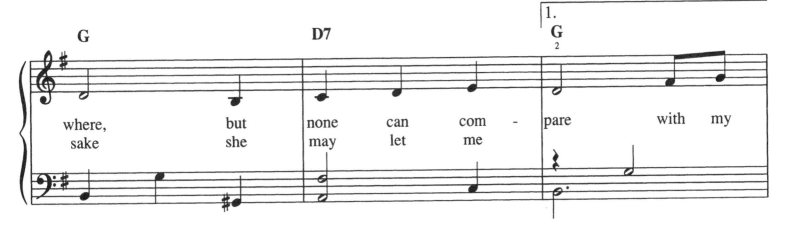

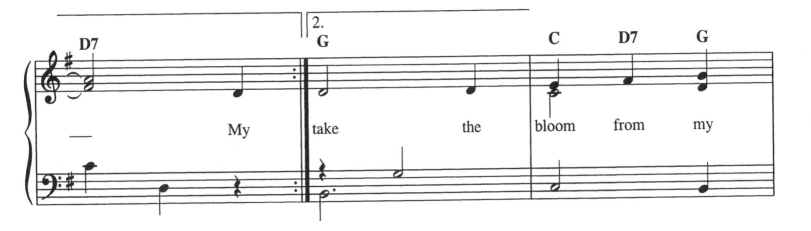

MOTHER MACHREE

Flowing, with expression

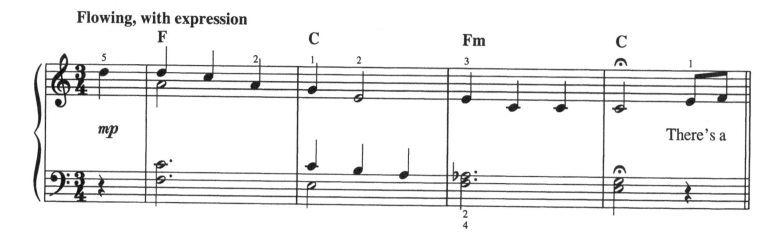

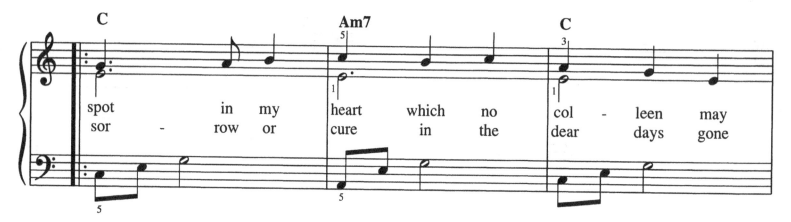

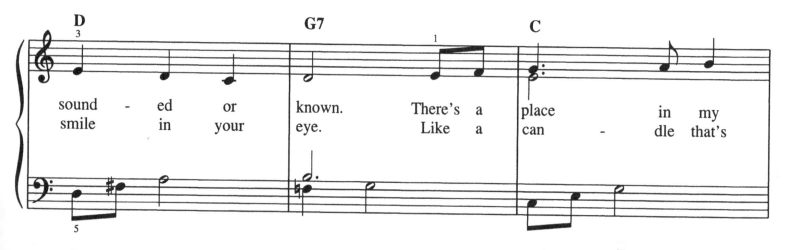

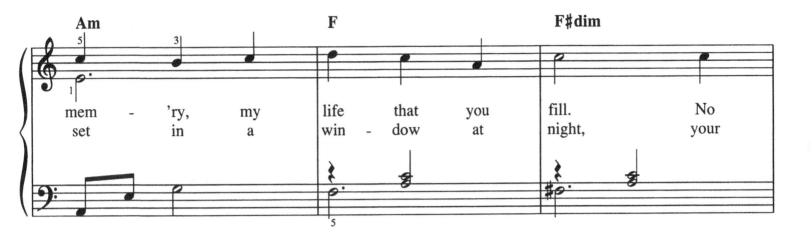

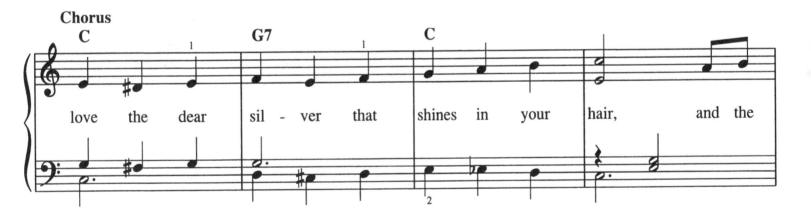

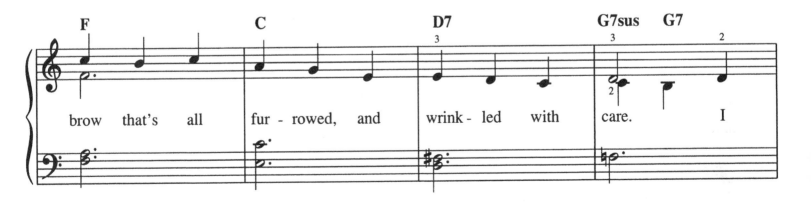

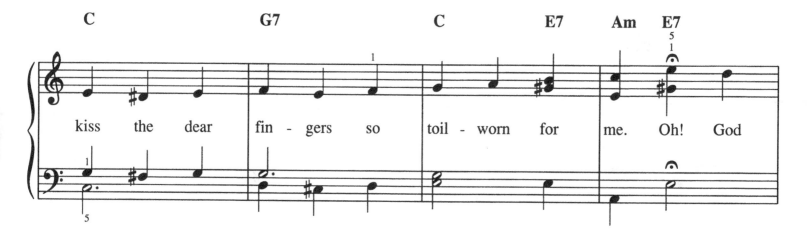

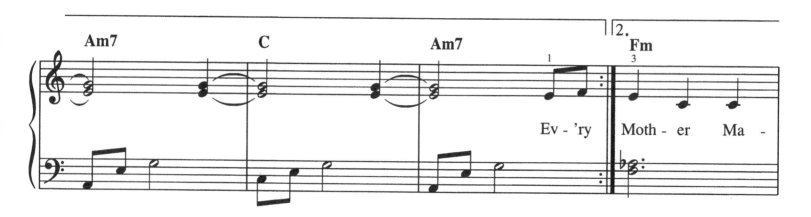

TOO - RA - LOO - RA - LOO - RAL
(That's An Irish Lullaby)

O - ver in Kil - lar - ney, _____
Off in dreams I wan - der, _____

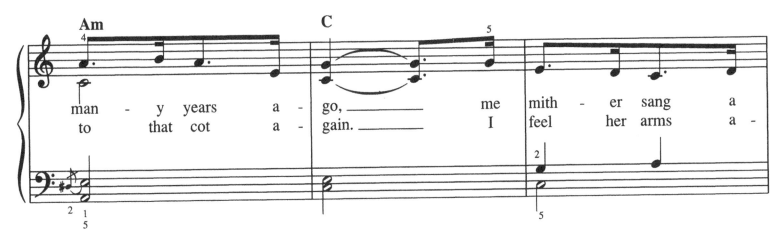

man - y years a - go, _____ me mith - er sang a -
to that cot a - gain. _____ I feel her arms a -

song to me in tones so sweet and low. Just a
hug - gin' me as when she held me then. And I

C ... **Am**

sim - ple lit - tle dit - ty, in her good ould I - rish
hear her voice a - hum-min' to me as in days of

C ... **F** ... **C**

way, and I'd give the world if she could sing that
yore, when I'd she used to rock me fast a - sleep out -

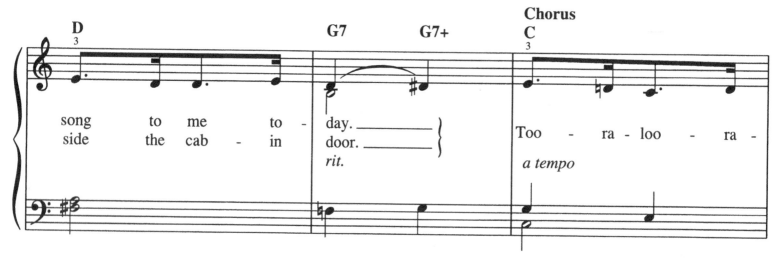

D ... **G7** **G7+** **Chorus** **C**

song to me to - day. _____
side the cab - in door. _____

rit.   *a tempo*

Too - ra - loo - ra -

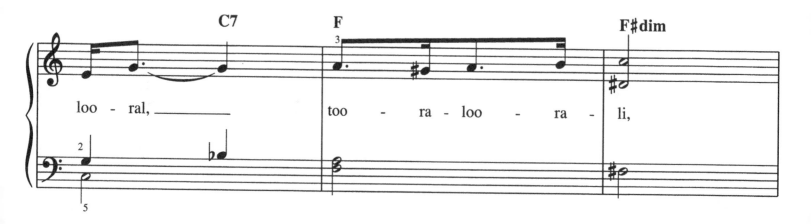

C7 ... **F** ... **F#dim**

loo - ral, _____ too - ra - loo - ra - li,

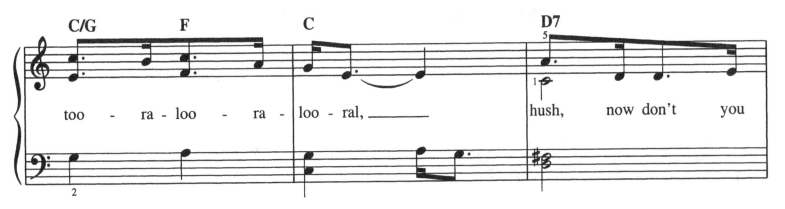

too - ra - loo - ra - loo - ral, _____ hush, now don't you

cry! _____ Too - ra - loo - ra - loo - ral, _____ too - ra - loo - ra -

li, too - ra - loo - ra - loo - ral, that's an I - rish lul - la -

by. loo - ral, that's an I - rish lul - la - by.

RORY O'MOORE

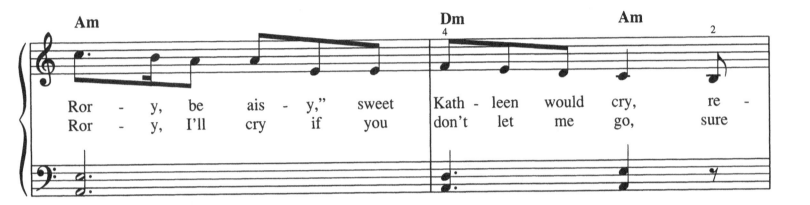

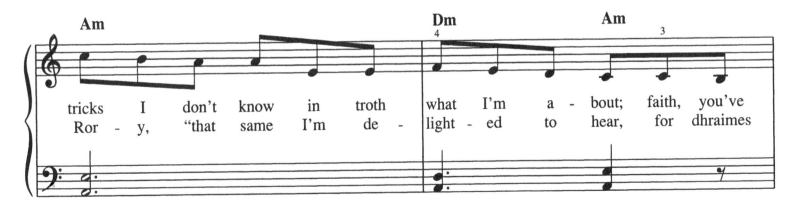

teas'd till I've put on my cloak in - side out." "O
al - ways go by con - thrair - ries, my dear. O

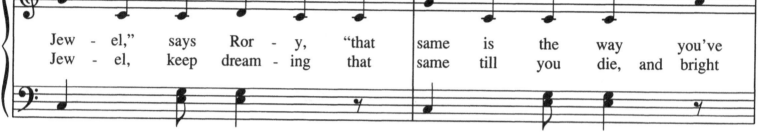

Jew - el," says Ror - y, "that same is the way you've
Jew - el, keep dream - ing that same till you die, and bright

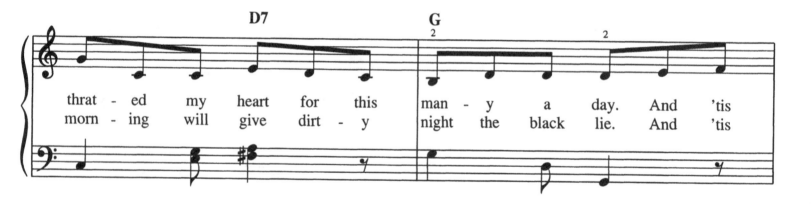

thrat - ed my heart for this man - y a day. And 'tis
morn - ing will give dirt - y night the black lie. And 'tis

pleas'd that I am and why not, to be sure? For 'tis
pleas'd that I am and why not, to be sure? Since 'tis

Additional Lyrics

3. "Arrah Kathleen, my darling, you've teas'd me enough,
And I've thrashed for your sake Dinny Grimes and Jim Duff.
And I've made myself drinking your health quite a baste,
So I think after that I may talk to the priest."
Then Rory the rogue stole his arm around her neck,
So soft and so white without freckle or speck.
And he look'd in her eyes that were beaming with light,
And he kiss'd her sweet lips, don't you think he was right?
"Now Rory, leave off, sir, you'll hug me no more,
That's eight times today that you've kiss'd me before."
"Then here goes another," says he, "to be sure,
For there's luck in odd numbers," says Rory O'Moore.

THE ROSE OF TRALEE

Sweetly

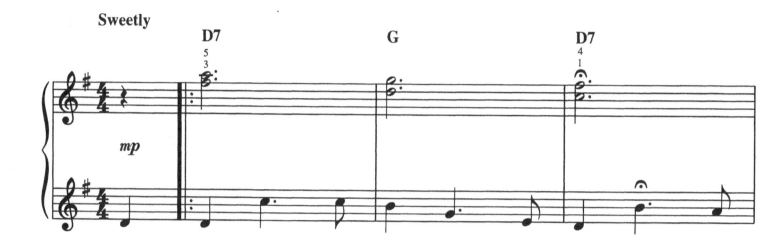

The pale moon was ris - ing a -
The cold shades of eve - ning their

bove the green moun - tain, the sun was de all
man - tle were spread - ing, and Ma - ry all

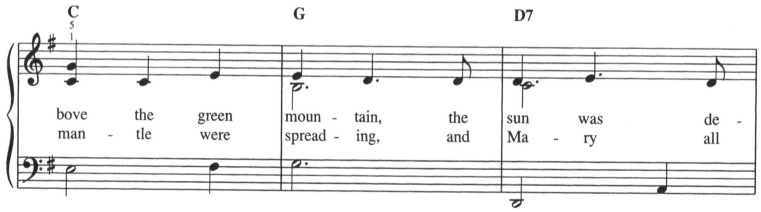

clin - ing be - neath the blue sea, when I
smil - ing was list - 'ning to me. The

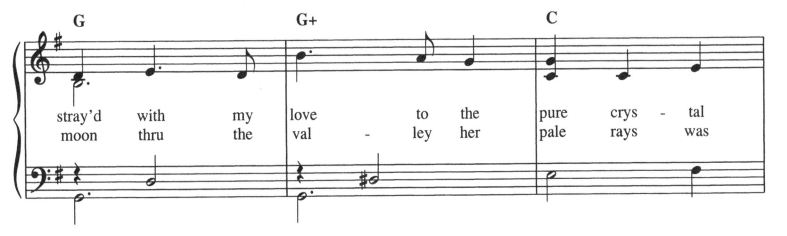

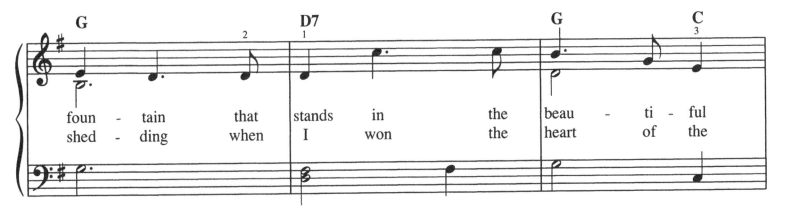

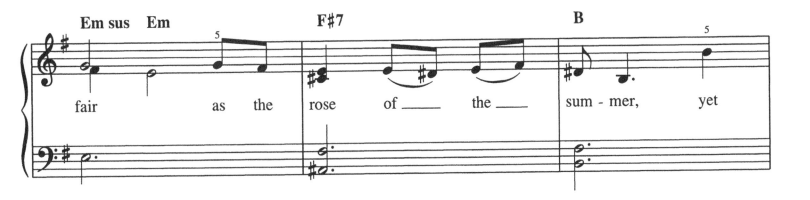

'twas not her beau - ty a -

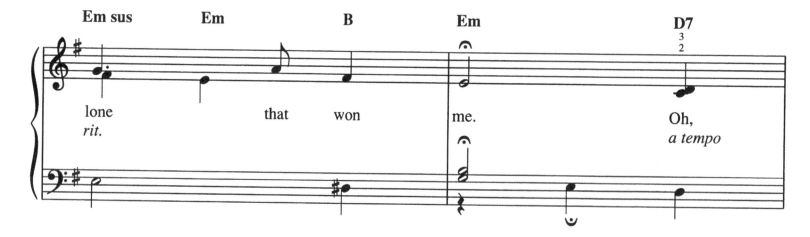

lone that won me. Oh,

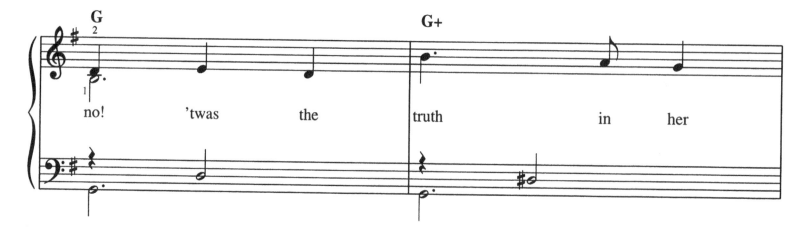

no! 'twas the truth in her

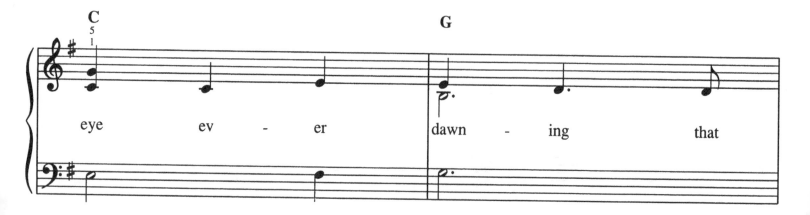

eye ev - er dawn - ing that

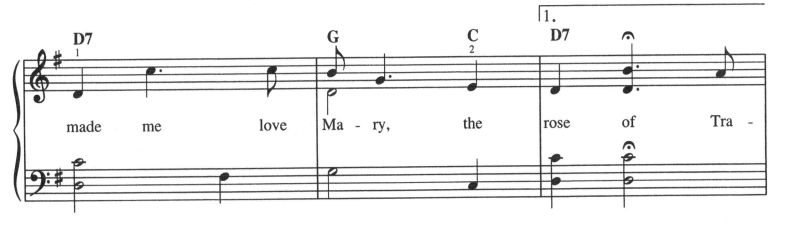

made me love Ma - ry, the rose of Tra -

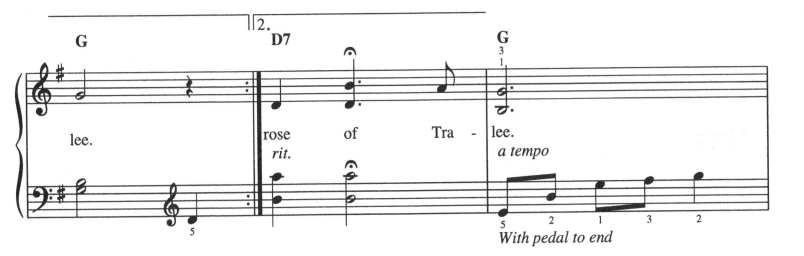

lee. rose of Tra - lee.

rit. *a tempo*

With pedal to end

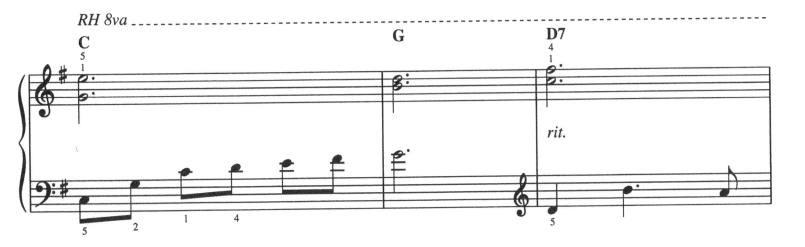

rit.

RH 8va

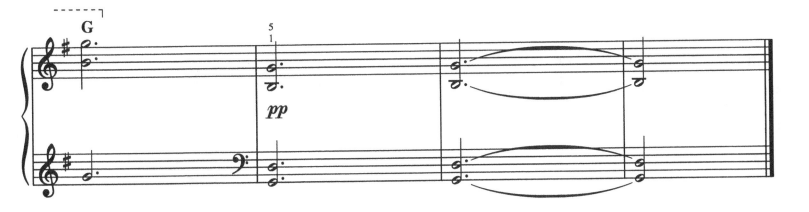

pp

SWEET ROSIE O'GRADY

Moderate waltz tempo

Sweet Ro - sie O' - Gra - dy,

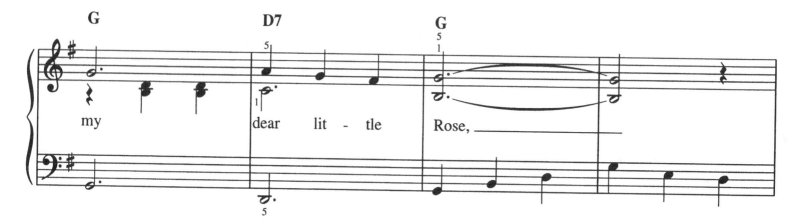

my dear lit - tle Rose, _____

she's my stead - y la - dy

most   ev - 'ry - one   knows. _____   And

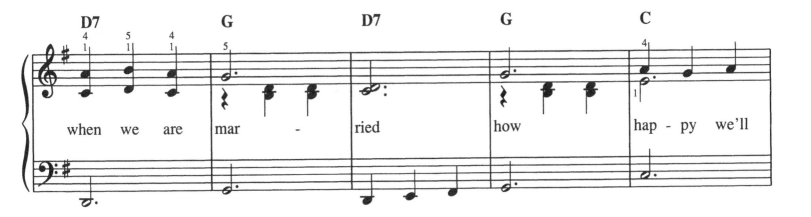

when we are   mar -   ried   how   hap - py we'll

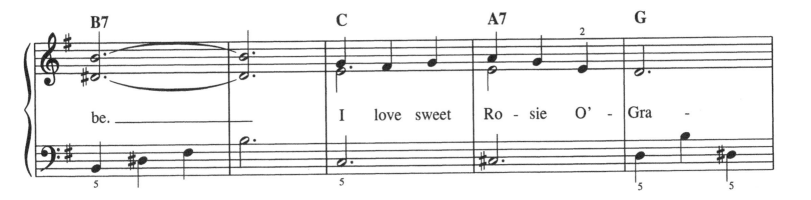

be. _____   I love sweet Ro - sie O' - Gra -

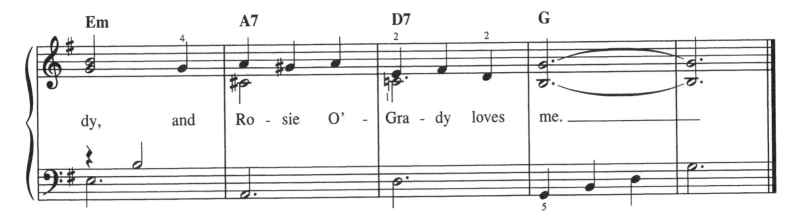

dy,   and   Ro - sie O' - Gra - dy loves   me. _____

'TIS THE LAST ROSE OF SUMMER

Slowly and tenderly

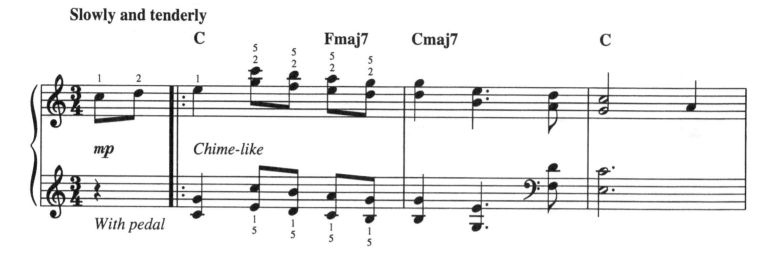

mp   *Chime-like*

With pedal

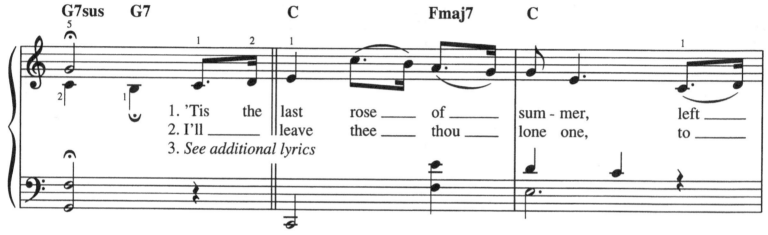

1. 'Tis the last rose ____ of ____ sum - mer, left ____
2. I'll ____ leave thee ____ thou ____ lone one, to ____
3. *See additional lyrics*

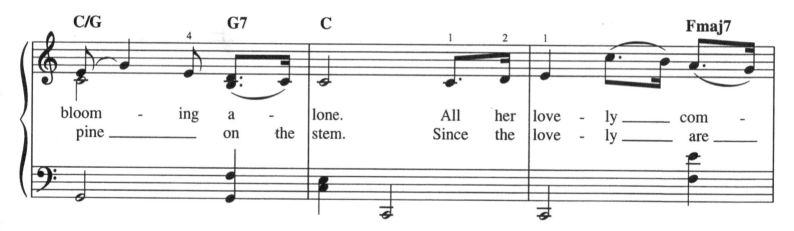

bloom - ing a - lone. All her love - ly ____ com -
pine ____ on the stem. Since the love - ly ____ are

pan - ions are ____ fad - ed and ____ gone. No ____
sleep - ing, go ____ sleep ____ thou with ____ them. Thus ____

Additional Lyrics

3. So soon may I follow, when friendships decay,
And from love's shining circle the gems drop away;
When true hearts lie withered, and fond ones are flown,
Oh, who would inhabit this bleak world alone.

TOURELAY

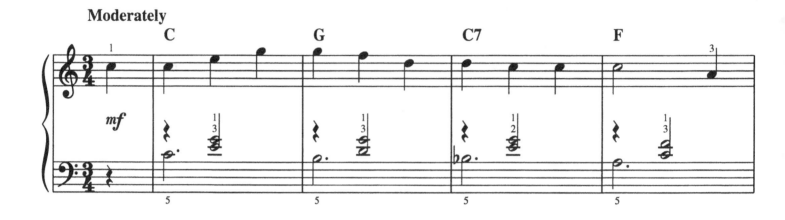

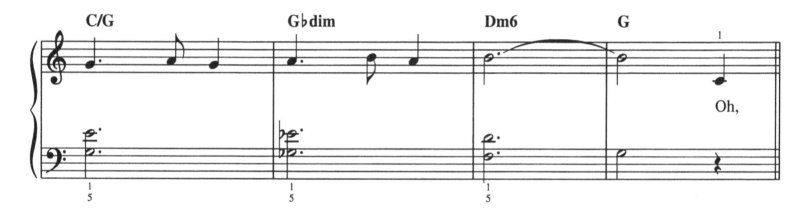

Oh,

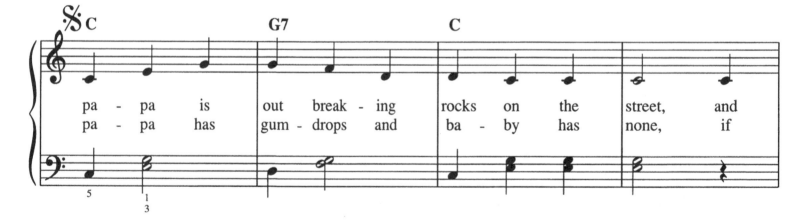

pa - pa is out break - ing rocks on the street, and
pa - pa has gum - drops and ba - by the has none, if

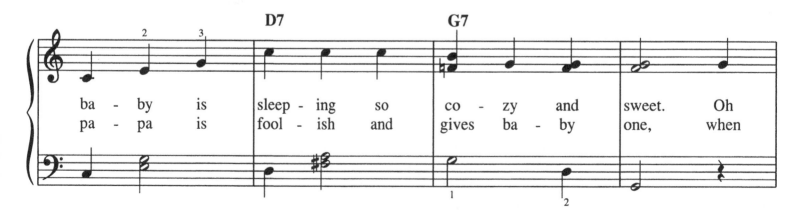

ba - by is sleep - ing so co - zy and sweet. Oh
pa - pa is fool - ish and gives ba - by one, Oh when

ba - by, don't cry now, but be ver - y good, and when
four o' - clock comes and but the child sleeps no more, then poor

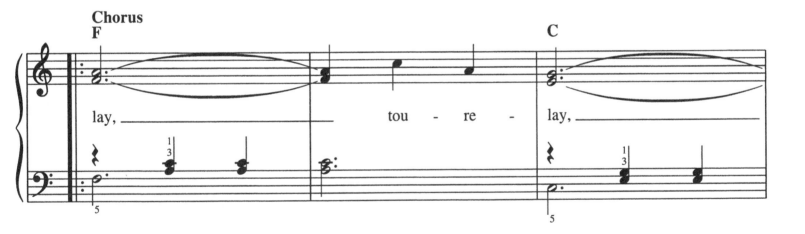

pa - pa comes home he'll bring you ci - ga - root. } Too - re -
pa - pa stays up all night pac - ing the floor. }

Chorus

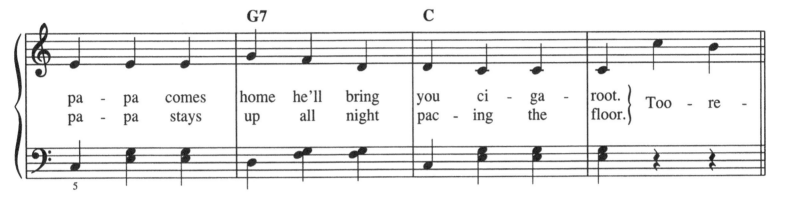

lay, _____ tou - re - lay, _____

_____ with my fil - la - ga du - sha, Shin - a - ma roo - sha, bal - der - al - da

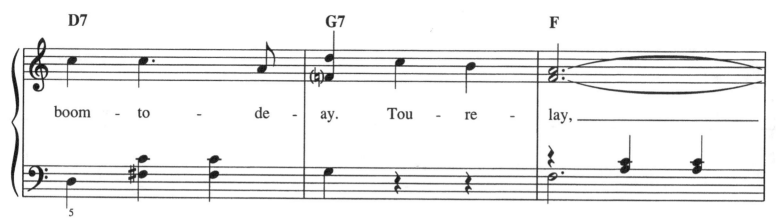

boom - to - de - ay. Tou - re - lay, _____

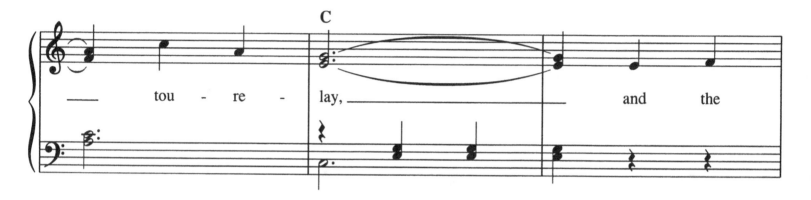

_____ tou - re - lay, _____ and the

To Coda ⊕

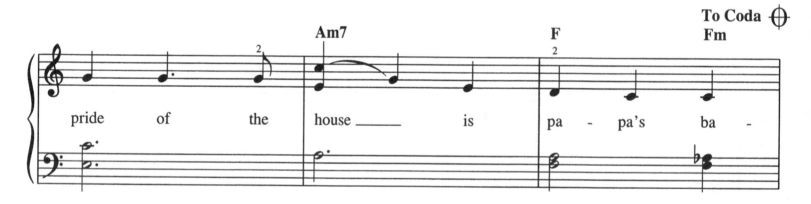

pride of the house _____ is pa - pa's ba -

D.S. al Coda
(with repeat)

CODA

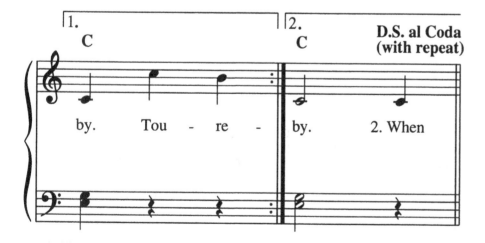

by. Tou - re -   by.   2. When

by.
rit.

WHEN IRISH EYES ARE SMILING

Moderate waltz tempo

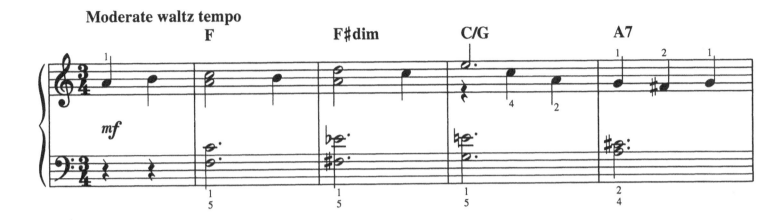

When

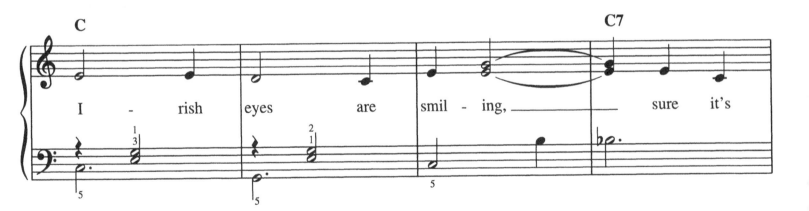

I - rish eyes are smil - ing, _____ sure it's

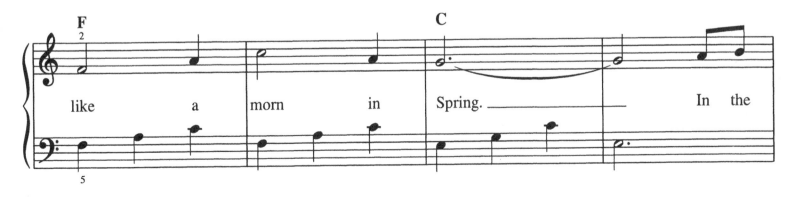

like a morn in Spring. _____ In the

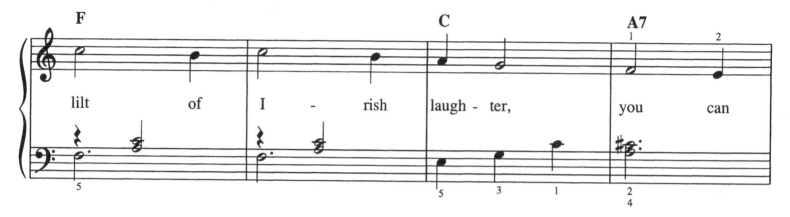

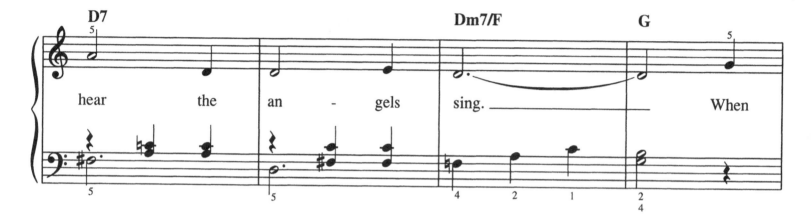

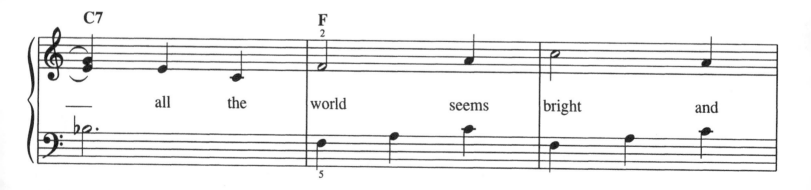

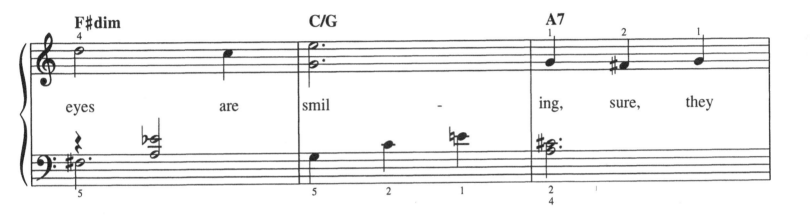

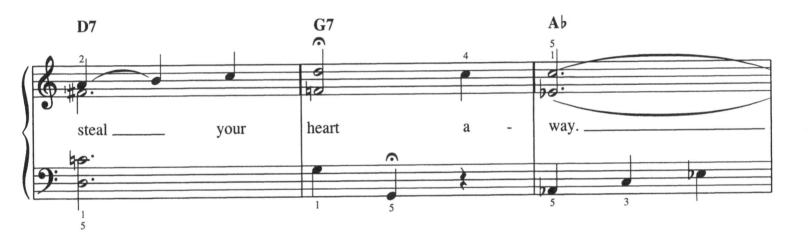

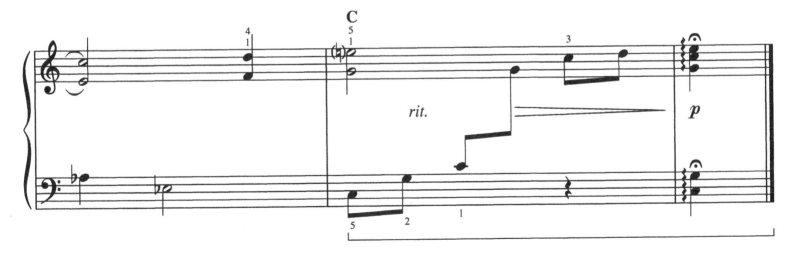

THE WEARIN' OF THE GREEN

Moderately

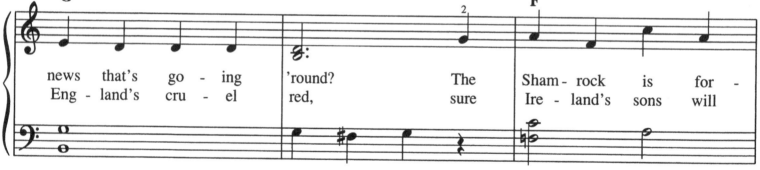

1. Oh, _____ Pad - dy dear, and did you hear the
2. since the co - lor we must wear is
3. *See additional lyrics*

news that's go - ing 'round? The Sham - rock is for -
Eng - land's cru - el red, sure Ire - land's sons will

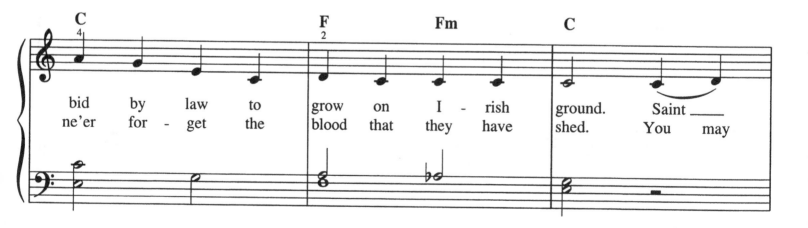

bid by law to grow on I - rish ground. Saint _____
ne'er for - get to blood that they have shed. You may

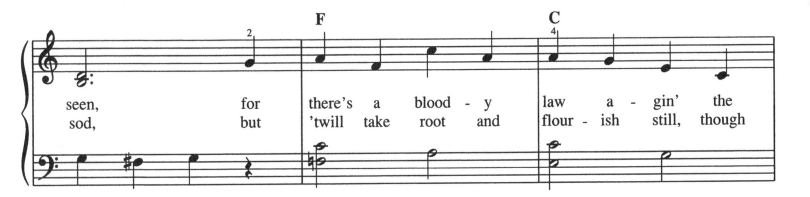

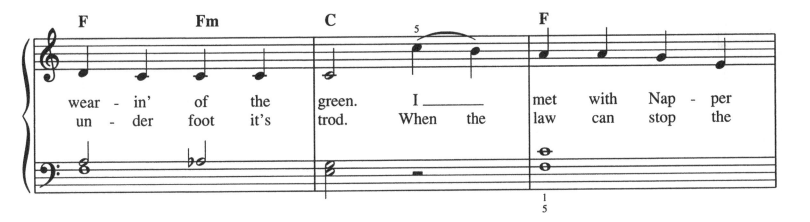

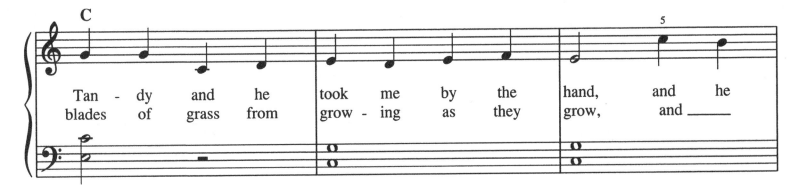

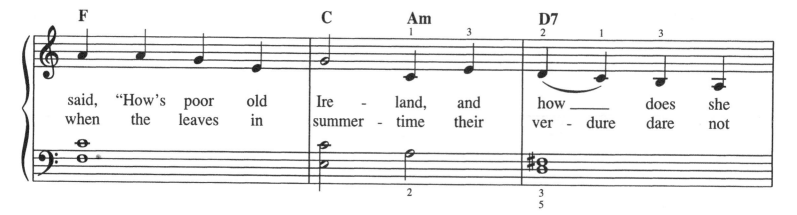

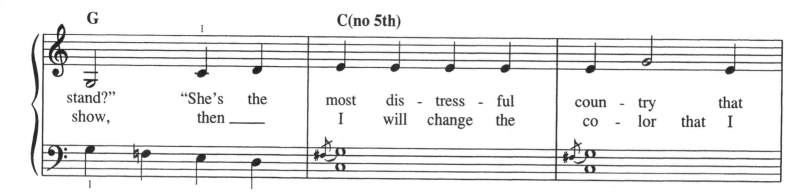

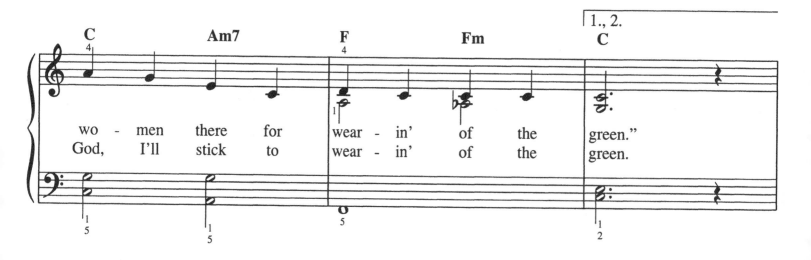

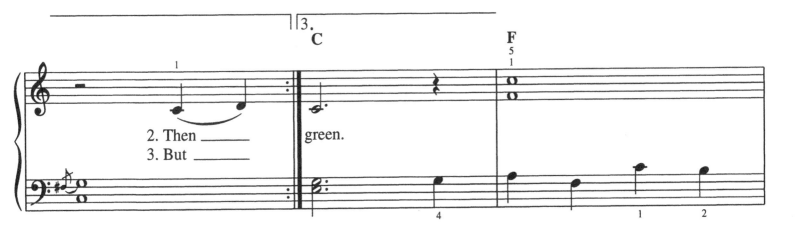

2. Then _____ green.
3. But _____

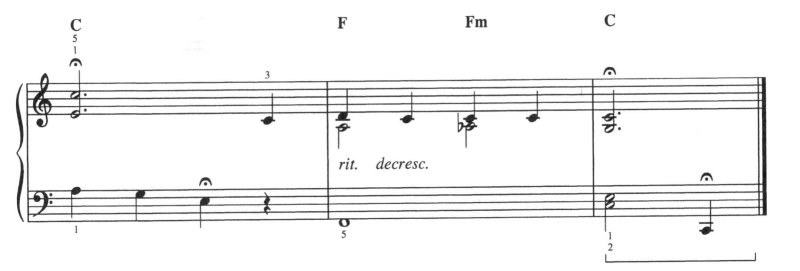

rit. decresc.

Additional Lyrics

3. But if, at last, our color should be torn from Ireland's heart,
Her sons, with shame and sorrow, from the dear old soil will part.
I've heard whisper of a country that lies far beyond the sea,
Where the poor stand equal in the light of freedom's day.

Oh, Erin, must we leave you, driven by the tyrant's hand?
Must we ask a mother's welcome from a strange but happier land?
Where the cruel cross of England's thraldom never shall be seen,
And where, thank God, we'll live and die still wearin' of the green.

WHO THREW THE OVERALLS IN MISTRESS MURPHY'S CHOWDER?

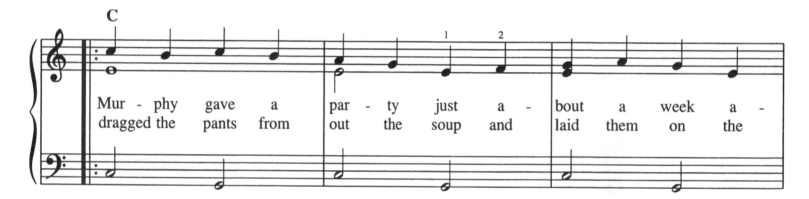

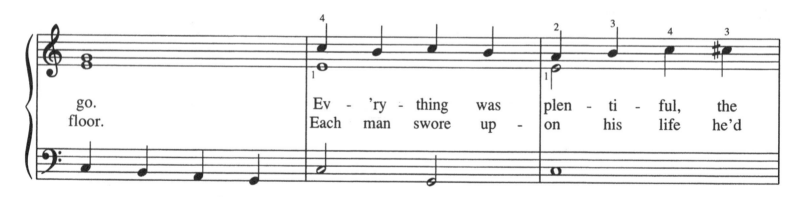

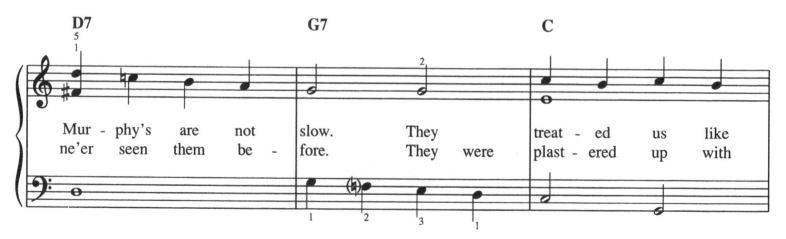

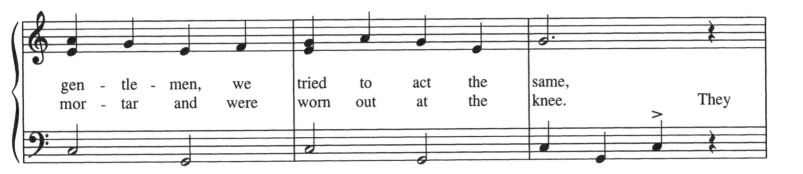

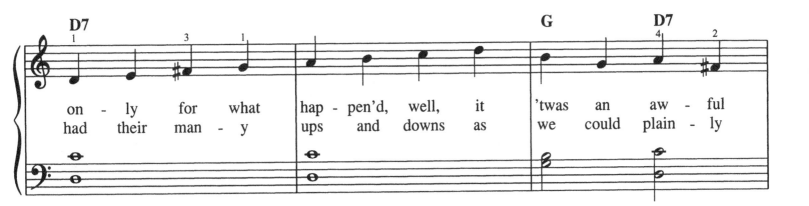

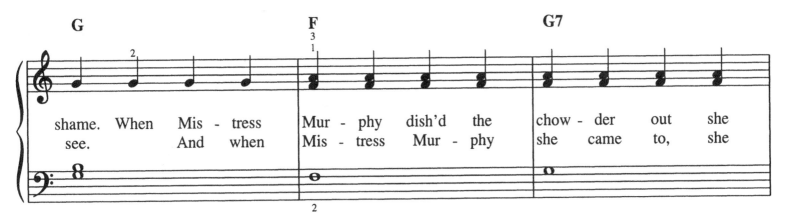

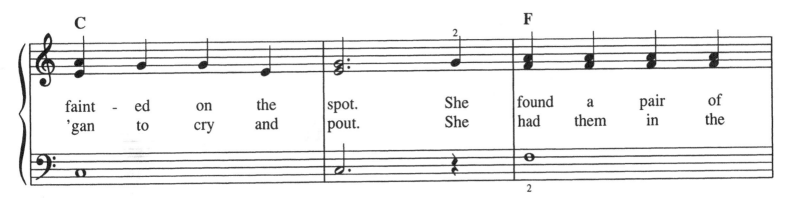

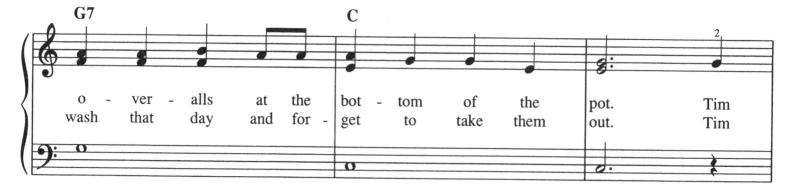

o - ver - alls at the bot - tom of the pot. Tim
wash that day and for - get to take them out. Tim

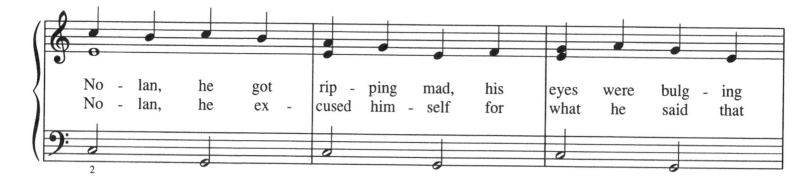

No - lan, he got rip - ping mad, his eyes were bulg - ing
No - lan, he ex - cused him - self for what he said that

out. He jump'd up on the pi - an - o and
night. So we put mu - sic to the words and

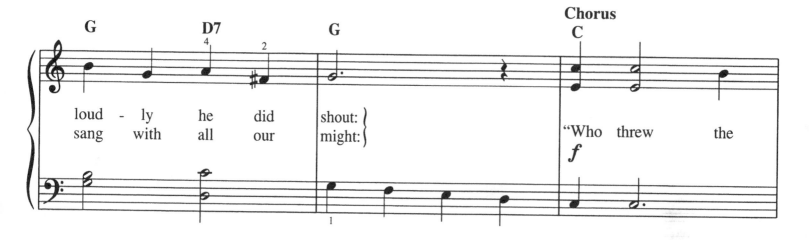

loud - ly he did shout:
sang with all our might:

"Who threw the

o - ver - alls in Mis - tress Mur - phy's chow-der?" No - bod - y

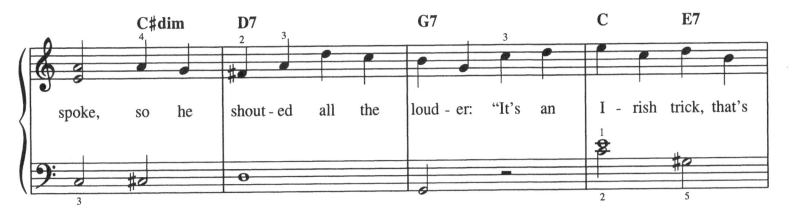

spoke, so he shout - ed all the loud - er: "It's an I - rish trick, that's

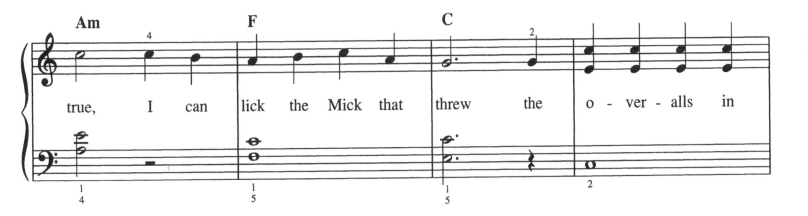

true, I can lick the Mick that threw the o - ver - alls in

Mis - tress Mur - phy's chow - der." They der."

WHERE THE RIVER SHANNON FLOWS

There's a pretty spot in Ire - land I al - ways claim for
Sure no let - ter I'll be mail - ing, for soon will I be

my land, where the fair - ies and the blar - ney will __
sail - ing, and I'll bless the ship the that takes me to my

nev - er nev - er die. It's the land of the shil -
dear old Er - in's shore. There I'll set - tle down for -

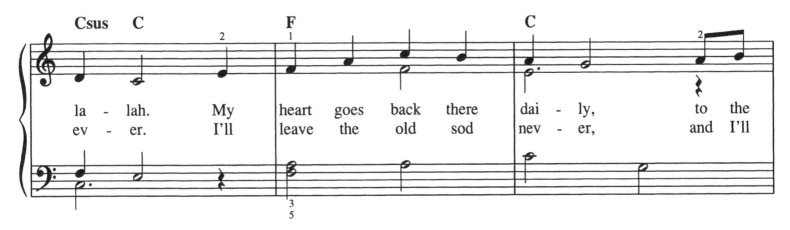

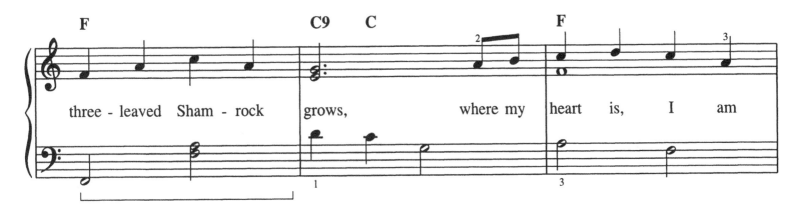

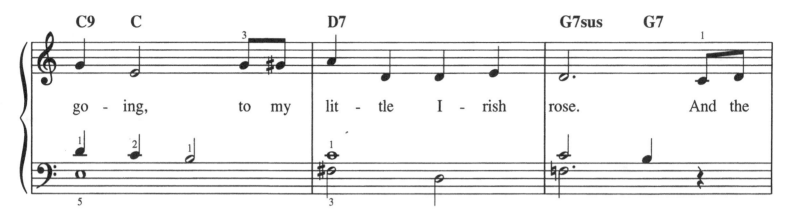

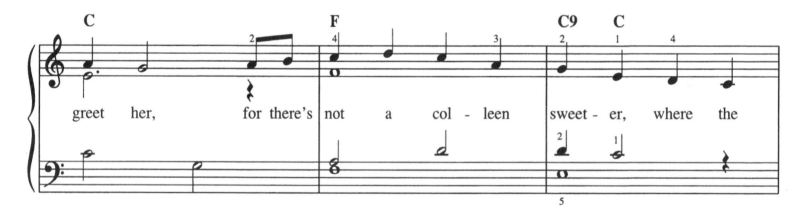

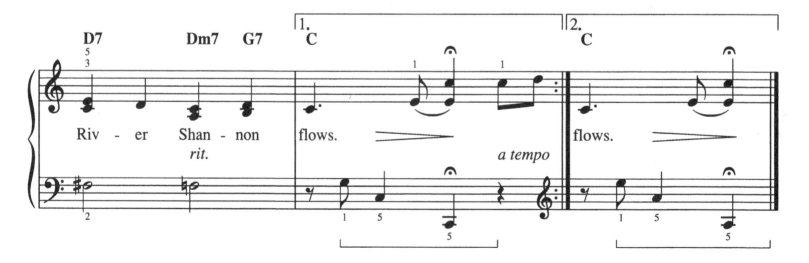